chocolate
divine indulgence

SCHOLASTIC

This edition published by Scholastic Inc., 557 Broadway, New York, NY 10012, by arrangement with McRae Publishing, Ltd.

Scholastic and associated logos are trademarks of Scholastic Inc.

Distributed by Scholastic Canada Ltd., Markham, Ontario

10 9 8 7 6 5 4 3 2

This book was conceived, edited and designed by McRae Publishing Ltd, London

Copyright © 2013 McRae Publishing Ltd

All rights reserved. Unauthorized reproduction, in any manner, is prohibited.

Project Director Anne McRae
Art Director Marco Nardi

Photography Brent Parker Jones
Text Carla Bardi, Ting Morris

Editing Christine Price, Anne McRae
Food Styling Lee Blaylock, Mark Hockenhull

Food Styling Assistant Rochelle Seator

Prop Styling Lee Blaylock
Layouts Aurora Granata

Prepress Filippo Delle Monache

ISBN 978-0-545-73870-5

Printed in Shanghai, China

PICTURE CREDITS:
All photographs by BRENT PARKER JONES except for the following:

17 Henri Gerbault, Poster advertising Carpentier chocolate, 1895 / Private Collection / The Stapleton Collection / The Bridgeman Art Library; 18 Firmin Bouisset, Poster advertising Menier chocolate, 1893 / Private Collection / The Stapleton Collection / The Bridgeman Art Library; 19t Menier chocolate factory, © Benh LIEU SONG; 20 Swiss School (19th Century), Poster advertising Suchard chocolate / Private Collection / Photo © Barbara Singer / The Bridgeman Art Library; 21 Steinlen, Poster advertising the Compagnie Francaise des Chocolats et des Thés, c. 1898 / Bibliothèque des Arts Decoratifs, Paris, France / Archives Charmet / The Bridgeman Art Library; 22b Shutterstock / msheldrake; 22t Shutterstock / PHB.cz (Richard Semik); 23b Shutterstock / Aaron Amat; 23t Shutterstock / Madlen; 23m Shutterstock / Picsfive.

NOTE TO OUR READERS
Eating eggs or egg whites that are not completely cooked poses the possibility of salmonella food poisoning. The risk is greater for pregnant women, the elderly, the very young, and persons with impaired immune systems. If you are concerned about salmonella, you can use reconstituted powdered egg whites or pasteurized eggs.

Carla Bardi & Ting Morris

chocolate
divine indulgence

contents

. . . . .
DON'T MISS

CHOCOLATE MINT CREAMS

CHOCOLATE CARAMEL SQUARES

CHOCOLATE BUTTERFLY CUPCAKES

CHOCOLATE MUD CAKE

TRUFFLE TEMPTATION

TRUFFLE TEMPTATION

At a Glance

This book has more than 150 recipes, ranging from cookies, brownies, and cupcakes, to cakes, pastries, and candy. On these pages you will find some ideas for unmissable, quick, classic, casual, favorite, novel, challenging, and celebratory dishes. Just to get you started!

. . . . .
EASY

MILK CHOCOLATE CHIP SHORTBREAD

NO-BAKE CHOCOLATE SQUARES

CHOCOLATE CAKE WITH BEETS

EASY PAN AU CHOCOLAT

EASY CHOCOLATE TART WITH PEARS

WHITE CHOCOLATE & RASPBERRY TIRAMISÙ

MINI CHOCOLATE CUPCAKES WITH RAINBOW FROSTING

SWEDISH RYE CAKE

IRISH CREAM FUDGE

CHOCOLATE HOKEY POKEY

OLD FAVORITES

CHECKERBOARD COOKIES

RUM & RAISIN BROWNIES

BLACK FOREST CUPCAKES

DEVIL'S FOOD CAKE

CHURROS WITH AZTEC SAUCE

CHOCOLATE MERINGUE PIE

CHILLED MUD CAKE WITH COFFEE CREAM

CASUAL ENTERTAINING

WHITE CHOCOLATE CHIP COOKIES WITH COCONUT

CHOCOLATE CHIP WEDGES

CHOCOLATE APPLE CAKE

CHOCOLATE PEAR GALETTES

COOL CHOCOLATE PIE

CHOCOLATE CHERRY DELIGHTS

BOOZY CHOCOLATE BERRY CAKE

QUICK

QUICK MARBLE CAKE

CHOCOLATE CHIP & OAT COOKIES

BRUNCH COOKIES

AZTEC BROWNIES

WHITE CHOCOLATE MUFFINS WITH PASSION FRUIT

CHOCOLATE ALMOND TORTE

FRUIT & NUT CHOCOLATE CANDY

CLASSICS

188

DOBOS TORTE

36

CHOCOLATE CHIP
COOKIES

82

CHOCOLATE MACADAMIA
BROWNIES

185

SACHERTORTE

225

PARIS-BREST

272

FROZEN MISSISSIPPI
MUD PIE

304

CHOCOLATE FUDGE

CELEBRATION

56

CHOCOLATE CHRISTMAS
COOKIES

112

CHOCOLATE MINT BARS

196

CHOCOLATE YULE LOG

200

CELEBRATION ROLL

254

CHILLED CHOCOLATE
ORANGE TORTE

300

COCONUT TRUFFLES

178

CHOCOLATE BIRTHDAY CAKE

CHALLENGING

182

PRINCE REGENT TORTE

180

ESTERHÁZY TORTE

186

BOSTON CREAM PIE

214

CHOCOLATE & VANILLA
CANNOLI

222

MINI CROQUEMBOUCHES
WITH SUGAR NETTING

262

MOZART BOMBE

314

CHOCOLATE EASTER
EGGS WITH SPRINKLES

SOMETHING SPECIAL

CHOCOLATE PANFORTE

FLORENTINE STARS

CHOCOLATE-DIPPED
BANANA KIPFERL

CHOCOLATE PEAR
MUFFINS

CHOCOLATE MINT
TRUFFLE CAKE

INNSBRUCK CHOCOLATE
NUT STRUDEL

RICOTTA CREAM PUFFS
WITH CHOCOLATE
FROSTING

CHOCOLATE ESPRESSO
TIRAMISÙ

WHITE CHOCOLATE CHEESE-
CAKE WITH RASPBERRY COULIS

CHOCOLATE PECAN
FUDGE

CHOCOLATE RICOTTA
SANDWICHES

CHOCOLATE MERINGUES
WITH BERRIES & CREAM

CHOCOLATE HAZELNUT
CUPCAKES

FROSTED MOCHA CAKE

CHOCOLATE TARTLETS
WITH RASPBERRIES

WHITE CHOCOLATE
TRIFLE

MILK CHOCOLATE
CHEESECAKE

CHOCOLATE MINT
HEARTS

WHITE CHOCOLATE
WALNUT FUDGE

EDITOR'S CHOICE

CHOCOLATE-DIPPED STRAWBERRIES

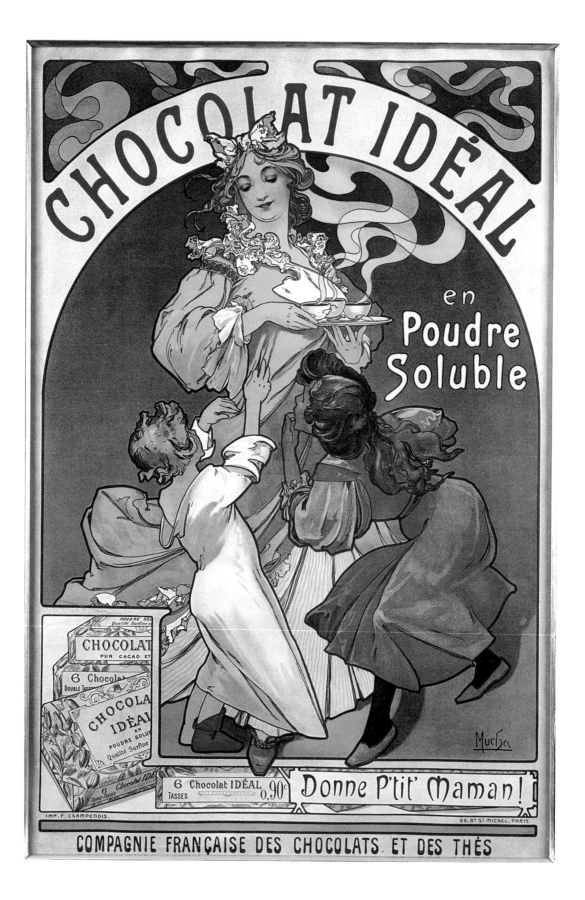

Divine Indulgence

The cacao plant was named *theobroma cacao* or "food of the gods," after an Aztec myth about Quetzalcoatl who was said to have stolen a cacao tree from his fellow gods in paradise. He took the beans to earth, traveling on a beam of the morning star, and gave them to the people of Mexico. Quetzalcoatl also taught the women how to roast and grind the beans to make a drink. The first Europeans in Central America seemed to confirm this tale when they described the women who made and sold "the drink of nobles," infused with chilies, vanilla, and honey.

Processing cacao beans into an edible substance is a complicated business, and the method seems to have been discovered by the Olmecs on the Mexican gulf coast some 3,500 years ago. They passed this skill onto the Mayas who succeeded them and who, in their turn, transferred the knowledge north, to the Aztecs.

For all the peoples of Mesoamerica, chocolate was more than just the main ingredient in some delicious

Above: A poster for Carpentier chocolate by French artist Henri Gerbault (1863–1930).

Opposite: A poster for Chocolat Idéal (1897), by the Czech Art Nouveau artist Alphonse Mucha (1860–1939).

drinks, porridges, and powders. It was deeply entwined with their culture and daily life, so much so that cacao beans were used as currency to acquire household goods and to pay laborers. There were festivals to celebrate the gods associated with cacao beans. Children were anointed in a ceremony similar to baptism with a liquid made from flowers and cacoa dissolved in water. Cacao beans were exchanged by the bride and groom at marriage ceremonies as symbols to seal their pact.

Christopher Columbus was the first European to lay eyes on cacao beans when he captured a Maya trading canoe loaded with merchandise near modern-day Honduras, in 1502. Columbus did not know what the strange-looking but obviously highly valued "almonds" in the cargo were, but it didn't take long for the Spanish conquistadors who followed him to understand their value.

Chocolate was soon taken to Europe, perhaps by Hernán Cortés. The first documented presence of chocolate occurs in 1544 when a delegation of Maya nobles traveled to Spain to meet with the future king, Philip II. Among the many gifts they bought were vessels filled with chocolate. Slow to catch on at first, the drink was prescribed as a medicine among the wealthy, some of whom must have developed cravings that they continued to assuage even after returning to

Above: The 19th century Menier Chocolate Factory in Noisiel, France.

Opposite: A poster for Menier Chocolate, by French artist Firmin Etienne Bouisset (1859–1925).

Above: A 19th century poster advertising Swiss Suchard Chocolate.

Opposite: A poster by Swiss Art Nouveau painter and printmaker Steinlen (1859-1923).

perfect health.

And so chocolate spread from Spain to Italy, France, and the rest of Europe. It journeyed with two other new drinks destined to become enormously popular—coffee and tea. Coffee-houses were established where many drinks were served, including hot chocolate, although chocolate remained an elite drink, a beverage for the discerning and well-off.

At this time too, chefs began to experiment with chocolate as a flavoring for sauces and other foods. In northern Italy, especially, chefs were exploring the possibilities of chocolate not only in cakes and other sweet preparations, but in pasta and meat dishes. Mesoamerican cooks did not use chocolate in their cooking and even though mole is considered a classic of Mexican cuisine, it was not invented until the 17th century. Today the word chocolate conjures up a delectable bar of solid, sweet, and usually milky substance; this is a fairly recent innovation, dating to the Industrial Revolution.

In this book we have gathered together more than 200 chocolate recipes. Our guiding principle has been to choose delicious recipes geared to the needs of busy home cooks who want "divine" chocolate dishes, without becoming martyrs or slaves to their kitchens. We hope

Types of Chocolate

Above: Milk chocolate makes up more than 80 percent of chocolate sales in the United States. As the health benefits of dark chocolate become better known, high quality dark chocolate sales are increasing yearly.

Chocolate can be divided into three broad types: dark chocolate, milk chocolate, and white chocolate. When baking, we also often use cocoa powder and, less commonly, chocolate liqueur.

COCOA POWDER Two types of cocoa powder are commonly used in baking: Dutch-processed cocoa, which has been treated with alkali to neutralize its acidity, and natural unsweetened cocoa powder, which has a more intense chocolate flavor.

DARK CHOCOLATE There are many types of dark chocolate, ranging from sweet and semisweet, to bittersweet and unsweetened.

MILK CHOCOLATE This chocolate is sweetened, contains milk, and usually has no more than 10–20 percent cocoa solids.

WHITE CHOCOLATE This chocolate is made with cocoa butter, sugar, milk, and vanilla. In some countries it cannot be labeled "chocolate" because it doesn't contain enough (or any) cocoa solids.

Right: Unsweetened cocoa powder is paler than the reddish brown Dutch-processed cocoa powder.

Dark chocolate is the most widely used in baking. The amount of cocoa solids in dark chocolate varies greatly, from about 30 percent in sweet dark chocolate to almost 100 percent in some very dark bars. However, remember that a very high amount of cocoa solids is no guarantee of quality. In our recipes we have used good-quality dark chocolate with cocoa content ranging from 50 to 70 percent.

Milk chocolate is creamier than dark chocolate and has a delicious flavor. In Europe, it must contain at least 25 percent cocoa solids. Milk chocolate is often used in baking.

White chocolate has a mild and pleasant flavor. Good quality white chocolate can be used in cookies, cakes, and desserts.

Basic Techniques

You don't need to be a professional pastry chef to make the recipes in this book. We have rated all the recipes at one of three levels: 1) Simple; 2) Medium; or 3) Challenging. If you are not an experienced cook, choose simple recipes to start with, then work your way up to the more challenging ones. You will also find that we have avoided recipes that require complicated, expensive, or unusual equipment. Our aim was to ensure that almost all the recipes could be made successfully in a reasonably well-equipped home kitchen. We have also avoided difficult chocolate techniques that most home cooks won't be able to manage; there are already many good books and internet videos to consult if you are interested in developing your skills.

For our recipes, you will only need to know how to melt chocolate, either in a double boiler or in the microwave, and how to create chocolate shavings and curls, and some simple chocolate leaves for decoration.

■ DECORATING WITH CHOCOLATE

a) Making Easy Shavings

1. Take a block of good quality chocolate. Soften slightly by zapping in the microwave for 5 seconds.

2. Hold the chocolate with a clean kitchen cloth and use a vegetable peeler to shave off small, thin shavings.

3. Cover with plastic wrap (cling film) or aluminum foil and chill the shavings until ready to use.

b) Making Chocolate Curls

1. Melt the chocolate completely, either in the microwave or double boiler (see pages 28–29).

2. Pour the chocolate onto a cold marble slab or, if you haven't got one of those, the back of a baking sheet.

3. Use a flat metallic spatula to spread the chocolate into a very thin layer.

c) Making Chocolate Leaves

1. Choose well rinsed, organic dried leaves. Make sure they are not toxic and have not been sprayed with chemicals. Rose leaves are a good choice.

2. Melt the chocolate, in the microwave or a double boiler (see pages 28–29). Use a small paintbrush to paint a thick coating on the underside of the leaves.

3. Place the leaves, chocolate-side-up, on a baking sheet lined with parchment paper. Chill in the refrigerator until set, about 15 minutes.

4. Place in the freezer for 1–2 minutes. Take out and press with a fingertip. When ready it should leave just a very light mark.

5. Use a broad, sharp-edged spatula to push along under the chocolate, rolling it into fat curls. If it is too cold the curls will break. Wait a few seconds and try again. If the chocolate gets too warm while you work, place in the freezer for a few seconds.

6. Place the chocolate curls on a plate, cover, and chill in the refrigerator until ready to use.

4. Paint with another layer of chocolate. Chill again.

5. Carefully peel off the leaves, leaving just the chocolate leaves.

6. Dust with unsweetened cocoa powder and store in the refrigerator until ready to use.

a) In the Microwave

You will need: A microwave-proof bowl and a metal spoon, or a silicone or rubber spatula, to stir.

1. Chop the chocolate with a large knife or coarsely grate; you will need fairly small pieces.

2. Put the chocolate in the microwave-proof bowl. Put in the microwave for 1 minute.

b) Double Boiler Method

You will need: A double boiler, with top and bottom pans, or a larger pan with a smaller pan or glass bowl that fits inside, without touching the water; a metal spoon or a silicone or rubber spatula to stir.

1. Coarsely chop the chocolate with a large knife (pieces can be larger than for the microwave method).

2. Fill the bottom of the double boiler or larger pan with water and bring to a gentle simmer.

3. Remove and stir with the metal spoon or rubber spatula.

4. Return to the microwave for short periods, 10–20 seconds each, stirring in between, until melted and smooth.

3. Put the chocolate in the top of the double boiler or in the smaller pan or glass bowl and place over the larger pan. The top pan or bowl should not be touching the water.

4. Leave until melted and smooth, stirring gently often. Be careful not to get water or condensation in the pan with the chocolate, otherwise it will seize.

cookies

This chapter features 24 cookie recipes, from classic Chocolate chip cookies and Checkerboard cookies, to melt-in-your-mouth Chocolate macaroons and meringues.

Makes: 16–20 large
   cookies
Preparation: 15 minutes
Cooking: 10–12 minutes
Level: 1

WHITE CHOCOLATE CHIP COOKIES
with coconut

2   cups (300 g) all-purpose (plain) flour

2   teaspoons baking powder

1/2   cup (50 g) unsweetened shredded (desiccated) coconut

1/2   cup (120 g) salted butter, softened

1   cup (200 g) sugar

1   teaspoon vanilla extract (essence)

1   large egg

1   cup (180 g) white chocolate chips

Preheat the oven to 350°F (180°C/gas 4). Line two large baking sheets with parchment paper.

Sift the flour and baking powder into a bowl. Stir in the coconut.

Beat the butter, sugar, and vanilla in a bowl with an electric mixer on medium-high speed until pale and creamy. Add the egg, beating until just combined. With the mixer on low speed, gradually add the flour mixture, beating until a soft dough forms. Stir in the chocolate chips by hand.

Scoop up heaped tablespoons of dough and roll into balls. Place on the prepared baking sheets, spacing about 2 inches (5 cm) apart. Flatten slightly.

Bake for 10–12 minutes, until pale golden brown. Rotate the baking sheets halfway through for even baking.

Let the cookies cool on the baking sheets for 2–3 minutes, until they are firm enough to move. Transfer to a wire rack and let cool completely.

. . .

If you liked this recipe, you will love these as well.

WHITE CHOCOLATE
SHORTBREAD WITH
CRANBERRIES

CHOCOLATE CHIP
COOKIES

WHITE CHOCOLATE
MACADAMIA COOKIES

MILK CHOCOLATE CHIP SHORTBREAD

1⅓ cups (200 g) all-purpose (plain) flour
2 tablespoons unsweetened cocoa powder
¼ teaspoon salt
¾ cup (180 g) unsalted butter, softened
½ cup (100 g) superfine (caster) sugar
½ cup (90 g) milk chocolate chips

Sift the flour, cocoa, and salt into a bowl. Beat the butter and sugar in a bowl with an electric mixer on medium-high speed until pale and creamy. With the mixer on low speed, gradually beat in the flour mixture. Stir in the chocolate chips by hand.

Divide the dough into two equal pieces. Shape each piece into a log about 2 inches (5 cm) thick. Wrap in plastic wrap (cling film) and chill for 1 hour.

Preheat the oven to 350°F (180°C/gas 4). Line a large baking sheet with parchment paper. Slice the logs into ½-inch (1-cm) thick rounds and place on the prepared baking sheet.

Bake for 10–12 minutes, until just firm. Rotate the baking sheet halfway through for even baking. Let cool completely on the baking sheet.

Makes: 12–14 cookies Preparation: 20 minutes + 1 hour to chill Cooking: 10–12 minutes Level: 1

WHITE CHOCOLATE SHORTBREAD
with cranberries

2 cups (300 g) all-purpose (plain) flour
½ teaspoon salt
1 cup (250 g) unsalted butter, softened
1 cup (150 g) confectioners' (icing) sugar
1 teaspoon vanilla extract (essence)
½ cup (75 g) dried cranberries, coarsely chopped
3½ ounces (100 g) white chocolate, finely chopped

Preheat the oven to 325°F (170°C/gas 3). Line two baking sheets with parchment paper. Sift the flour and salt into a bowl.

Beat the butter, confectioners' sugar, and vanilla in a bowl with an electric mixer on medium-high speed until pale and creamy. Stir in the flour mixture, cranberries, and chocolate chips.

Roll tablespoonfuls of the dough into balls. Place on the prepared baking sheets, spacing about 2 inches (5 cm) apart. Use a fork to flatten slightly. Chill in the refrigerator for 15 minutes.

Bake for 15–18 minutes, until pale golden brown. Rotate the baking sheets halfway through for even baking. Let cool completely on the baking sheets.

Makes: 28–30 cookies Preparation: 20 minutes + 15 minutes to chill Cooking: 15–18 minutes Level: 1

Shortbread is a classic Scottish cookie, traditionally made with one part sugar, two parts butter, and three parts flour. Its high fat content gives it a crumbly texture and a delicious, rich flavor. There are many variations on the classic recipe.

This shortbread is enriched with dried cranberries, also known as "craisins." Dried cranberries contain antioxidants that are believed to help prevent heart disease and some types of cancer.

Makes: 45–50 large
  cookies
Preparation: 20 minutes
  + 1 hour to chill
Cooking: 15–20 minutes
Level: 1

. . . . .

Classic chocolate chip cookies were invented by accident in Massachusetts in the 1930s. When restaurant owner and chef Ruth Wakefield ran out of baker's chocolate she replaced it in her cookies with chunks of semisweet chocolate that did not melt during baking. The cookies were so delicious that they quickly became a hit.

CHOCOLATE CHIP COOKIES

3	cups (450 g) all-purpose (plain) flour
1½	teaspoons baking soda (bicarbonate of soda)
½	teaspoon salt
1¼	cups (310 g) unsalted butter, softened
1½	cups (300 g) firmly packed light brown sugar
1	cup (200 g) sugar
1½	teaspoons vanilla extract (essence)
3	large eggs
1	pound (500 g) dark chocolate chips

Sift the flour, baking soda, and salt into a large bowl.

Beat the butter, both sugars, and vanilla in a large bowl with an electric mixer on medium-high speed until creamy. Add the eggs one at a time, beating until just combined after each addition.

With the mixer on low speed, gradually beat in the flour mixture. Stir in the chocolate chips by hand. Cover the bowl and chill for 1 hour.

Preheat the oven to 350°F (180°C/gas 4). Line three or four large baking sheets with parchment paper.

Scoop up heaped tablespoons of dough and roll into balls. Place on the prepared baking sheets, spacing about 3 inches (7 cm) apart.

Bake for 15–20 minutes, until the cookies are golden brown at the edges but still very soft in the center. Rotate the sheets halfway through for even baking.

Let the cookies cool on the baking sheets for 2–3 minutes, until they are firm enough to move. Transfer to a wire rack and let cool completely.

. . .

If you liked this recipe, you will love these as well.

WHITE CHOCOLATE CHIP
COOKIES WITH COCONUT

MILK CHOCOLATE CHIP
SHORTBREAD

CHOCOLATE CHIP
WEDGES

. . . . .

These cookies should be slightly under-baked so that they are soft and chewy. If you prefer a crisper cookie, bake for 2–3 minutes longer, until deep golden brown.

CHOCOLATE CHIP & OAT COOKIES

1   cup (100 g) old-fashioned rolled oats

1   cup (150 g) all-purpose (plain) flour

1/2   teaspoon baking soda (bicarbonate of soda)

1/2   teaspoon baking powder

1/2   teaspoon salt

2   ounces (60 g) milk chocolate, grated

1/2   cup (120 g) unsalted butter, softened

1/2   cup (100 g) firmly packed dark brown sugar

1/2   cup (100 g) sugar

1   large egg

1/2   teaspoon vanilla extract (essence)

3/4   cup (135 g) dark chocolate chips

Preheat the oven to 375°C (190°C/gas 5). Line a large baking sheet with parchment paper.

Put the oats into a food processor and chop to a fine powder. Add the flour, baking soda, baking powder, and salt and process well. Add the grated chocolate.

Beat the butter and both sugars in a bowl with an electric mixer on medium-high speed until creamy. Beat in the egg and vanilla. With the mixer on low speed, gradually beat in the chocolate chips and flour mixture.

Roll into balls the size of walnuts and place 2 inches (5 cm) apart on the prepared baking sheet.

Bake for 10–12 minutes, until pale golden brown. Rotate the baking sheet halfway through for even baking.

Let the cookies cool on the baking sheets for 2–3 minutes, until they are firm enough to move. Transfer to a wire rack and let cool completely.

. . .

If you liked this recipe, you will love these as well.

WHITE CHOCOLATE CHIP
COOKIES WITH COCONUT

WHITE CHOCOLATE
SHORTBREAD WITH
CRANBERRIES

BRUNCH COOKIES

WHITE CHOCOLATE MACADAMIA COOKIES

2½	cups (375 g) all-purpose (plain) flour
1	teaspoon baking powder
1	cup (250 g) salted butter, softened
1	cup (200 g) firmly packed light brown sugar
½	cup (100 g) sugar
2	teaspoons vanilla extract (essence)
2	large eggs
¾	cup (90 g) chopped macadamia nuts
6	ounces (180 g) white chocolate, coarsely chopped

Preheat the oven to 350°F (180°C/gas 4). Line three large baking sheets with parchment paper. Sift the flour and baking powder into a bowl.

Beat the butter, both sugars, and vanilla in a bowl with an electric mixer on medium-high speed until creamy. Add the eggs one at a time, beating until just combined after each addition. With the mixer on low speed, gradually beat in the flour mixture. Stir in the macadamias and white chocolate by hand.

Drop heaped tablespoons of the dough onto the prepared baking sheets, spacing 2 inches (5 cm) apart. Bake for 12–15 minutes, until light golden brown and firm to the touch. Rotate the baking sheets halfway through for even baking.

Let the cookies cool on the baking sheets for 2–3 minutes, until they are firm enough to move. Transfer to a wire rack and let cool completely.

Makes: 40–45 cookies Preparation: 15 minutes Cooking: 12–15 minutes Level: 1

BRUNCH COOKIES

1	cup (150 g) all-purpose (plain) flour
½	cup (75 g) whole-wheat flour
½	teaspoon baking soda
¾	cup (180 g) salted butter, softened
1	cup (200 g) packed light brown sugar
1	large egg
1½	teaspoons vanilla
1	banana, mashed
1	cup (100 g) old-fashioned rolled oats
8	ounces (250 g) dark chocolate, chopped
½	cup (60 g) walnuts

Preheat the oven to 375°F (190°C/gas 5). Line two large baking sheets with parchment paper. Sift both flours and the baking soda into a bowl.

Beat the butter and brown sugar in a bowl with an electric mixer on medium-high speed until creamy. Add the egg and vanilla extract, beating until just combined. With the mixer on low speed, add the banana and flour mixture, beating until just combined. Stir in the oats, chocolate, and coarsely chopped walnuts by hand.

Drop heaped tablespoons of dough onto the prepared baking sheets, spacing about 2 inches (5 cm) apart. Bake for 12–15 minutes, until golden brown and firm to the touch. Rotate the baking sheets halfway through for even baking.

Let the cookies cool on the baking sheets for 2–3 minutes, until they are firm enough to move. Transfer to a wire rack and let cool completely.

Makes: 30–35 cookies Preparation: 15 minutes Cooking: 12–15 minutes Level: 1

Crisp, buttery macadamias are native to Australia. They are high in healthy monounsaturated fat, and are an excellent source of thiamine. They contain useful amounts of minerals, such as manganese and selenium, and a host of antioxidants.

Serve these cookies with coffee at breakfast or brunch for an energy-packed start to the day.

Makes: 16–20 cookies
Preparation: 20 minutes
Cooking: 14–16 minutes
Level: 1

CHOCOLATE THUMBPRINT COOKIES

³/₄ cup (120 g) all-purpose (plain) flour

¹/₂ cup (75 g) whole-wheat (wholemeal) flour

¹/₂ teaspoon baking soda (bicarbonate of soda)

¹/₄ teaspoon salt

1 cup (120 g) walnuts

¹/₄ cup (60 g) unsalted butter, softened

¹/₄ cup (60 ml) walnut oil or canola oil

¹/₂ cup (100 g) sugar

¹/₂ cup (100 g) firmly packed light brown sugar

1 large egg

2 teaspoons vanilla extract (essence)

5 ounces (150 g) dark chocolate, chopped

6 tablespoons apricot preserves (jam)

Preheat the oven to 375°F (190°C/gas 5). Line two large baking sheets with parchment paper.

Sift both flours, the baking soda, and salt into a bowl. Grind the walnuts in a food processor until they resemble coarse meal. Stir into the flour mixture.

Beat the butter, oil, and both sugars in a large bowl with an electric mixer on medium-high speed until creamy. Beat in the egg and vanilla. With the mixer on low speed, gradually beat in the flour mixture and chocolate.

Roll tablespoons of the dough into balls and place on the prepared baking sheets, spacing about 2 inches (5 cm) apart.

Bake the cookies for 6 minutes. Remove from the oven and gently press your gloved thumb or a wooden spoon into the center of each cookie to make a hollow. Place 1 teaspoon of apricot preserves in each hollow. Bake for 8–10 minutes more, until the preserves are melted and the cookie is set but still a little soft. Rotate the baking sheets halfway through for even baking.

Let the cookies cool on the baking sheets for 2–3 minutes, until they are firm enough to move. Transfer to a wire rack and let cool completely.

. . .

If you liked this recipe, you will love these as well.

CHOCOLATE CHIP & OAT COOKIES

WHITE CHOCOLATE MACADAMIA COOKIES

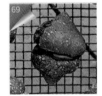

CHUNKY CHOCOLATE MACAROONS

Makes: 16–20 cookies
Preparation: 15 minutes
    + 1 hour to chill
Cooking: 10–12 minutes
Level: 1

You must chill the dough for at least an hour. Make sure it is well-wrapped in plastic wrap (cling film) so that it doesn't absorb other flavors from the refrigerator. You can leave it in the refrigerator for 2–3 days before baking, or freeze it for up to one month.

TRIPLE CHOCOLATE BUTTER COOKIES

Cookies
$1^{1}/_{3}$	cups (200 g) all-purpose (plain) flour
$^{1}/_{4}$	cup (30 g) unsweetened cocoa powder
$^{1}/_{4}$	teaspoon salt
$^{3}/_{4}$	cup (180 g) unsalted butter, softened
$^{1}/_{2}$	cup (100 g) sugar
$^{1}/_{2}$	cup (90 g) dark chocolate chips

Glaze
3	ounces (90 g) white chocolate

Cookies: Sift the flour, cocoa, and salt into a bowl. Beat the butter and sugar in a bowl with an electric mixer on medium-high speed until pale and creamy. With the mixer on low speed, gradually beat in the flour mixture.

Stir in the chocolate chips by hand. The dough will be very thick and crumbly. Squeeze it together in a ball with your hands.

Divide the dough into two equal pieces. Roll each piece into a log about 2 inches (5 cm) in diameter. Wrap in plastic wrap (cling film) and chill in the refrigerator for at least 1 hour.

Preheat the oven to 350°F (180°C/gas 4). Line two large baking sheets with parchment paper.

Slice the logs into $^{1}/_{2}$-inch (1-cm) thick rounds. Transfer to the prepared baking sheets, spacing about 2 inches (5 cm) apart.

Bake for 10–12 minutes. Rotate the baking sheets halfway through for even baking. Let the cookies cool completely on the baking sheets.

Glaze: Melt the white chocolate in a double boiler over barely simmering water, or in the microwave. Drizzle over the cooled cookies in a zig zag pattern. Let set before serving.

. . .

If you liked this recipe, you will love these as well.

MILK CHOCOLATE CHIP SHORTBREAD

CHOCOLATE-DIPPED BANANA KIPFERL

CHOCOLATE DRIPPERS

Makes: 20–24 cookies

Preparation: 30 minutes
+ 1½ hours to cool
& set

Cooking: 10–12 minutes

Level: 3

. . . . .

Florentines are a classic Italian cookie made with almonds and candied cherries set in caramel and covered with chocolate. In our recipe, we bake the cookie base in one piece, which allows us to spread it with a good thick layer of chocolate. You will need a sturdy metallic cookie cutter to cut out the cookies. You could also just use a large knife and cut the cookie into squares.

FLORENTINE STARS

Cookies

¾ cup (150 g) firmly packed light brown sugar

⅓ cup (90 ml) clear honey

¾ cup (180 g) salted butter

1 cup (100 g) unsweetened shredded (desiccated) coconut

1 cup (120 g) flaked almonds

1¾ cups (300 g) candied (glacé) cherries, coarsely chopped

4 tablespoons all-purpose (plain) flour

Glaze

8 ounces (250 g) dark chocolate

Cookies: Preheat the oven to 400°F (200°C/gas 6). Line a large baking sheet with parchment paper.

Combine the brown sugar, honey, and butter in a saucepan and melt over low heat. When the sugar has dissolved, stir in the coconut, flaked almonds, candied cherries, and flour.

Spread the mixture out on the prepared baking sheet in a thin layer. Don't worry if there are small gaps, they will melt together in the oven.

Bake for 10–12 minutes, until a rich golden color. Rotate the sheet halfway through for even baking.

Let cool completely on the baking sheet, about 1 hour.

Glaze: Melt the chocolate in a double boiler over barely simmering water, or in the microwave.

Line another large baking sheet with parchment paper and carefully flip the cooled large "cookie" onto it. Peel off the baking parchment. Spread with the melted chocolate. Let rest until set, about 30 minutes.

Use a star-shaped metallic cookie cutter to stamp out the cookies. You will need to press down hard on the cookie to press through the crisp, cooked cookie dough. If liked, rest a small plate or pan on top of the cookie cutter and push down on this instead.

. . .

If you liked this recipe, you will love these as well.

CHOCOLATE-DIPPED
BANANA KIPFERL

CHOCOLATE CHRISTMAS
STARS

FLORENTINE CUPCAKES

· · · · ·

This recipe makes a lot of these classic cookies. You may need to bake them in several batches, depending on your oven. They will keep in an airtight container for several days.

CHECKERBOARD COOKIES

1	cup (250 g) unsalted butter, softened
1/2	cup (100 g) sugar
1	teaspoon vanilla extract (essence)
1/2	teaspoon lemon extract (essence)
1/4	teaspoon salt
2 1/2	cups (375 g) all-purpose (plain) flour
3	tablespoons unsweetened cocoa powder
1	large egg
1	tablespoon cold water

Beat the butter and sugar in a bowl with an electric mixer on medium-high speed until pale and creamy. Add the vanilla extract, lemon extract, and salt. With the mixer on low speed, gradually beat in the flour.

Turn the dough out onto a clean work surface. It will be quite crumbly. Squeeze together in a ball and knead for 1 minute. Divide the dough into two equal pieces. Sprinkle the cocoa powder over one piece and knead until it has been fully incorporated.

Put each piece of dough between two sheets of plastic wrap (cling film). Using a rolling pin, shape the dough into two 7-inch (18-cm) squares. Using a sharp knife and a ruler, slice one square into nine 3/4-inch (2-cm) wide strips.

Beat the egg and water in a cup or small bowl. Cover the work surface with plastic wrap. Place three strips of dough side by side on the plastic wrap, alternating plain and chocolate strips. Brush the tops and in between the strips with egg wash. Gently press the strips together. Repeat, forming second and third layers, alternating the colors to create a checkerboard pattern. Wrap the resulting log in plastic wrap.

Repeat the process with the other piece of dough to make a second log, reversing the color pattern. Chill in the refrigerator 30 minutes.

Preheat the oven to 350°F (180°C/gas 4). Line three large baking sheets with parchment paper. Slice each log into 1/4-inch (5-mm) thick slices. Place on the prepared baking sheets, spacing about 1 inch (2.5 cm) apart.

Bake for 10–12 minutes. Rotate the baking sheets halfway through for even baking.

Let the cookies cool on the baking sheets for 2–3 minutes, until they are firm enough to move. Transfer to a wire rack and let cool completely.

. . . . .

Kipferl are small crescent-shaped cookies from Austria, Germany, the Czech Republic, and Hungary. According to legend, they are baked in the shape of the Islamic crescent to celebrate an important victory of the Hungarian army over the Turks.

CHOCOLATE-DIPPED BANANA KIPFERL

Cookies

$1^2/_3$	cups (250 g) all-purpose (plain) flour
1	teaspoon baking powder
$^1/_4$	teaspoon salt
$^2/_3$	cup (150 g) unsalted butter, softened
$^1/_2$	cup (100 g) sugar
1	large egg yolk
1	vanilla pod
1	cup (100 g) broken-up, dried, unsweetened banana chips

Glaze

5	ounces (150 g) dark chocolate, coarsely chopped

Cookies: Sift the flour, baking powder, and salt into a medium bowl. Beat the butter and sugar in a bowl with an electric mixer on medium-high speed until pale and creamy. Add the egg yolk, beating until just blended. Scoop out the seeds from the vanilla pod and add to the mixture.

With the mixer on low speed, gradually beat in the flour mixture and banana chips.

Divide the dough into two equal pieces. Form into 10-inch (25-cm) logs, wrap in plastic wrap (cling film), and refrigerate for 30 minutes.

Preheat the oven to 350°F (180°C/gas 4). Line three large baking sheets with parchment paper.

Cut the dough into $^1/_2$-inch (1-cm) thick slices. Press the centers inward and pull the ends around to form crescents. Place 1 inch (2.5 cm) apart on the prepared baking sheets.

Bake for 10–12 minutes, until just golden at the edges. Rotate the sheets halfway through for even baking.

Let the cookies cool on the baking sheets for 2–3 minutes, until they are firm enough to move. Transfer to racks and let cool completely.

Glaze: Melt the chocolate in a double boiler over barely simmering water, or in the microwave. Dip the end of each cookie into the chocolate. Let stand on parchment paper for 30 minutes to set.

. . .

If you liked this recipe, you will love these as well.

TRIPLE CHOCOLATE
BUTTER COOKIES

FLORENTINE STARS

CHOCOLATE DRIPPERS

Makes: 12–15 large
    cookies
Preparation: 25 minutes
    + 1½ hours to chill
    & set
Cooking: 12–15 minutes
Level: 1

CHOCOLATE DRIPPERS

Cookies

1	cup (150 g) all-purpose (plain) flour
²/₃	cup (100 g) cake flour
½	teaspoon baking powder
¼	teaspoon salt
2	large eggs
¾	cup (150 g) sugar
½	cup (120 ml) milk
⅓	cup (90 g) unsalted butter, melted and cooled
½	teaspoon vanilla extract (essence)
½	teaspoon lemon extract (essence)

Frosting

2	cups (300 g) confectioners' (icing) sugar, sifted
3	tablespoons boiling water
2	tablespoons light corn (golden) syrup
2	ounces (60 g) dark chocolate

Cookies: Preheat the oven to 350°F (180°C/gas 4). Line a large baking sheet with parchment paper.

Sift both flours, the baking powder, and salt into a bowl.

Beat the eggs and sugar in a bowl with an electric mixer on medium speed until pale and thick. Add the milk, beating to combine.

With the mixer on low speed, beat in the melted butter, vanilla and lemon extracts, and flour mixture to form a smooth dough. Chill for 1 hour.

Drop 12–15 scoops of dough onto the prepared baking sheet, spacing 2 inches (5 cm) apart.

Bake for 12–15 minutes, until the edges are pale golden brown. Rotate the baking sheet halfway through for even baking.

Let the cookies cool on the baking sheet for 2–3 minutes, until they are firm enough to move. Transfer to a wire rack and let cool completely.

Frosting: Combine the confectioners' sugar, water, and corn syrup in a bowl and whisk until smooth. Drizzle half the frosting over one half of each cookie. Return the cookies to the wire rack to drip.

Melt the chocolate in a double boiler over barely simmering water, or in the microwave. Stir into the remaining frosting until smooth. Drizzle the chocolate frosting over the other half of each cookie. Let sit until the frosting has set, about 30 minutes.

. . .

If you liked this recipe, you will love these as well.

TRIPLE CHOCOLATE
BUTTER COOKIES

FLORENTINE STARS

CHOCOLATE-DIPPED
BANANA KIPFERL

Makes: 30 cookies

Preparation: 30 minutes + 45 minutes to chill & set

Cooking: 14–18 minutes

Level: 1

CHOCOLATE CHRISTMAS STARS

Cookies

3/4 cup (180 g) unsalted butter, chilled, chopped

1/4 cup (30 g) unsweetened cocoa powder

1/3 cup (50 g) rice flour

1 cup (150 g) all-purpose (plain) flour

1/4 teaspoon salt

1 cup (150 g) confectioners' (icing) sugar + extra, to dust

2 teaspoons vanilla extract (essence)

Chocolate Ganache

1/2 cup (90 g) milk chocolate melts

1 tablespoon heavy (double) cream

Cookies: Chop the butter, cocoa, both flours, salt, and confectioners' sugar in a food processor until the mixture resembles bread crumbs. Add the vanilla and process until the mixture comes together. Shape into a disk, wrap in plastic wrap (cling film), and chill for 30 minutes.

Preheat the oven to 350°F (180°C/gas 4). Line three baking sheets with parchment paper.

Roll the dough out to 1/8 inch (3 mm) thick. Use a 1 1/2-inch (4-cm) star-shaped cutter to cut out 30 stars. Return the remaining dough to the refrigerator. Place the stars on one of the prepared baking sheets, spacing 1 inch (2.5 cm) apart.

Bake for 6–8 minutes, until the edges are just firm to the touch. Let the cookies cool on the baking sheet for 2–3 minutes, until they are firm enough to move. Transfer to a wire rack and let cool completely.

Roll out the remaining dough. Use a 2-inch (5-cm) star-shaped cutter to cut out 30 stars. Place on the remaining prepared baking sheets, spacing 1 inch (2.5 cm) apart.

Bake for 8–10 minutes, until the edges are just firm. Rotate the baking sheets halfway through for even baking.

Let the cookies cool on the baking sheets for 2–3 minutes, until they are firm enough to move. Transfer to a wire rack and let cool completely.

Chocolate Ganache: Melt the chocolate and cream in a double boiler over barely simmering water until smooth. Alternatively, place the chocolate and cream in a microwave-safe bowl. Microwave on high for 30 seconds, stirring halfway through, until melted and smooth. Set aside for 10 minutes to cool slightly.

Spoon some chocolate ganache on each large star cookie. Top with the small stars, pressing down gently. Set aside for 15 minutes to set. Dust with confectioners' sugar just before serving.

Makes: 28–30 cookies
Preparation: 15 minutes
Cooking: 12–14 minutes
Level: 1

. . . . .

Christmas mint lentils are chocolate mint candies coated in red, green, and white candy. You can buy them from well-stocked kitchen supply stores or from online suppliers.

CHOCOLATE CHRISTMAS COOKIES

1   cup (150 g) all-purpose (plain) flour
1/2 cup (75 g) unsweetened cocoa powder
1/2 teaspoon baking soda (bicarbonate of soda)
1/2 teaspoon salt
4   ounces (120 g) dark chocolate, chopped
1/2 cup (120 g) salted butter, cut into pieces
1 1/2 cups (300 g) sugar
2   large eggs, lightly beaten
1   teaspoon vanilla extract (essence)
1   cup Christmas Mint Lentils

Preheat the oven to 325°F (170°C/gas 3). Line two large baking sheets with parchment paper.

Sift the flour, cocoa, baking soda, and salt into a bowl. Melt the chocolate and butter in a double boiler over barely simmering water, or in the microwave. Let cool for 5 minutes.

Add the sugar, eggs, and vanilla to the melted chocolate mixture and beat with a wooden spoon until well combined, shiny, and smooth. Add the flour mixture, stirring until incorporated.

Stir in three-quarters of the mint lentils, setting the rest aside for later. Roll tablespoons of dough into balls and place on the prepared baking sheets, spacing about 2 inches (5 cm) apart, and flattening slightly. Press some of the reserved mint lentils into the top of each cookie.

Bake for 12–14 minutes, until spread and just firm to the touch. Rotate the baking sheets halfway through for even baking.

Let the cookies cool on the baking sheets for 2–3 minutes, until they are firm enough to move. Transfer to a wire rack and let cool completely.

. . .

If you liked this recipe, you will love these as well.

FLORENTINE STARS

CHOCOLATE CHRISTMAS STARS

CHOCOLATE YULE LOG

Makes: about 32 cookies
Preparation: 30 minutes
    + 15 minutes to cool
Cooking: 30–40 minutes
Level: 2

. . . . .

Biscotti are a classic Italian cookie. They are named for their cooking method; biscotti means "cooked twice" in Italian.

CHOCOLATE PISTACHIO BISCOTTI

1   cup (200 g) sugar

2   cups (300 g) all-purpose (plain) flour

1½ teaspoons baking powder

¼   teaspoon salt

¾   cup (120 g) shelled unsalted pistachios

4   ounces (120 g) dark chocolate, chopped

3   large eggs

2   tablespoons unsalted butter, melted

1   teaspoon vanilla extract (essence)

¼   cup (30 g) unsweetened cocoa powder

Preheat the oven to 350°F (180°C/gas 4). Line three large baking sheets with parchment paper and sprinkle with 2 tablespoons of the sugar.

Combine the flour, ¾ cup (150 g) of the remaining sugar, the baking powder, and salt in a bowl. Stir in the pistachios and chocolate.

Beat the eggs, butter, vanilla, and cocoa in a bowl with an electric mixer on medium speed until well mixed. Add the egg mixture to the flour mixture and stir until well combined. The dough will be quite stiff, so use your hands to finish mixing it.

Divide the dough into two equal pieces. Shape into two 2½ x 8-inch (6 x 20-cm) logs and place on one of the prepared baking sheets. Sprinkle with the remaining sugar.

Bake for 15–20 minutes, until just firm to the touch. Let the chocolate logs cool on the baking sheet for 15 minutes.

Reduce the oven temperature to 300°F (150°C/gas 2). Using a serrated knife, cut the logs crosswise into ½-inch (1-cm) thick slices. Arrange the slices on the remaining prepared baking sheets, spacing about 1 inch (2.5 cm) apart.

Bake for 15–20 minutes, until the biscotti are dry to the touch. Rotate the baking sheets halfway through for even baking.

Let the cookies cool on the baking sheets for 2–3 minutes, until they are firm enough to move. Transfer to a wire rack and let cool completely.

. . .

If you liked this recipe, you will love these as well.

WHITE CHOCOLATE MACADAMIA COOKIES

FLORENTINE STARS

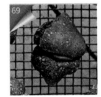

CHUNKY CHOCOLATE MACAROONS

Makes: 15–18 filled
    cookies
Preparation: 30 minutes
    + 15 minutes to chill
Cooking: 10–12 minutes
Level: 1

CHOCOLATE RICOTTA SANDWICHES

Cookies

1	cup (150 g) all-purpose (plain) flour
$1/4$	cup (30 g) finely ground almonds
$1/2$	cup (75 g) unsweetened cocoa powder
1	teaspoon baking soda (bicarbonate of soda)
$1/4$	teaspoon baking powder
$1/4$	teaspoon salt
$1^1/2$	cups (300 g) sugar
$3/4$	cup (180 g) unsalted butter
1	large egg

Filling

$1/2$	cup (120 g) fresh ricotta cheese
4	ounces (120 g) cream cheese
1	tablespoon sugar
1	teaspoon freshly squeezed lemon juice
1	teaspoon vanilla extract (essence)

Cookies: Preheat the oven to 375°F (190°C/gas 5). Line two large baking sheets with parchment paper.

Place the flour, almonds, cocoa, baking soda, baking powder, salt, and sugar in the bowl of a food processor. Add the butter and egg and process until the dough comes together as a soft dough.

Wrap the dough in plastic wrap (cling film) and chill for 15 minutes.

Roll tablespoons of the dough into balls and place on the prepared baking sheets, spacing about 2 inches (5 cm) apart, and flattening slightly.

Bake for 10–12 minutes, until firm to the touch. Rotate the baking sheets halfway through for even baking.

Let the cookies cool on the baking sheets for 2–3 minutes, until they are firm enough to move. Transfer to a wire rack and let cool completely.

Filling: Combine the ricotta, cream cheese, sugar, lemon juice, and vanilla in a bowl. Mix with a wooden spoon until creamy and smooth.·

Put a dollop of filling in the centers of half the cookies. Cover with the remaining cookies, pressing down gently, and serve.

. . .

*If you liked this recipe,
you will love these as well.*

CHOCOLATE MOUSSE
SANDWICHES

CHOCOLATE MINT
CREAMS

CHOCOLATE MACAROONS

Makes: 12 filled cookies
Preparation: 45 minutes
  + 1 hour to chill
Cooking: 8–10 minutes
Level: 2

· · · · ·

These little cookies make an elegant dessert.
Prepare an hour or two ahead of time and chill
in the refrigerator until ready to serve.

CHOCOLATE MOUSSE SANDWICHES

Cookies
- ½ cup (75 g) all-purpose (plain) flour
- ¼ cup (30 g) confectioners' (icing) sugar
- 3 tablespoons unsweetened cocoa powder
- 1 tablespoon ground almonds
- 3 tablespoons salted butter, cold and diced
- 1 large egg, lightly beaten

Mousse
- 12 ounces (350 g) dark chocolate, finely grated
- 2 cups (500 ml) heavy (double) cream
- Confectioners' (icing) sugar, to dust

Glaze
- ⅓ cup (120 g) apricot preserves (jam)
- 2 tablespoons water
- 6–8 whole fresh strawberries, with stems

Cookies: Sift the flour, confectioners' sugar, and cocoa into a bowl. Stir in the almonds. Add the butter and rub in with your fingertips until the mixture resembles fine crumbs.

Make a well in the center and pour in the egg a little at a time, mixing with your fingers until the dough comes together but is not sticky. You may not need all the egg. Dust with flour and wrap in plastic wrap (cling film). Chill for 30 minutes.

Mousse: Place the chocolate in a large heatproof bowl. Bring 1¼ cups (310 ml) of the cream to a boil over medium heat. Pour over the chocolate. Stir until melted and smooth. Transfer to a smaller bowl, cover with plastic wrap (cling film) and chill until cool, about 30 minutes.

Whip the remaining cream until thick. Fold into the cooled chocolate mixture. Chill until needed.

Preheat the oven to 350°F (180°C/gas 4). Line two large baking sheets with parchment paper.

Roll out the cookie dough to ¼ inch (5 mm) thick. Use a fluted 2-inch (5-cm) cookie cutter to cut out 24 disks. Place on the prepared baking sheets, spacing 1 inch (2.5 cm) apart.

Bake for 8–10 minutes, until firm to the touch. Rotate the baking sheets halfway through for even baking.

Let the cookies cool on the baking sheets for 2–3 minutes, until they are firm enough to move. Transfer to a wire rack and let cool completely.

Glaze: Heat the apricot preserves gently over low heat. Whisk in the water and remove from the heat. Take a strawberry by the stem and dip into the preserves. Set aside on a plate. Dip each strawberry in the same way. Remove the stems and slice thickly.

Spoon the mousse into a pastry (piping) bag with a star nozzle. Place a cookie on a plate and pipe a spiral of mousse on top. Cover with another cookie. Dust lightly with confectioners' sugar and top with a slice of strawberry. Repeat with the remaining cookies, mousse, and strawberries.

Makes: 18–20 filled
   cookies
Preparation: 45 minutes
   + 1½ hours to chill
Cooking: 8–10 minutes
Level: 2

. . . . .

Add some pizazz to these cookies by stirring a few drops of green food coloring into the filling.

CHOCOLATE MINT CREAMS

Cookies

1	cup (150 g) all-purpose (plain) flour
2	tablespoons unsweetened cocoa powder
⅛	teaspoon salt
½	cup (120 g) unsalted butter, softened
¼	cup (50 g) sugar
1	teaspoon mint extract (essence)
1	large egg

Filling

½	cup (120 ml) heavy (double) cream
8	ounces (250 g) white chocolate, grated
1	teaspoon mint extract (essence)

Glaze

5	ounces (150 g) dark chocolate, coarsely chopped
⅓	cup (90 g) salted butter

Cookies: Sift the flour, cocoa, and salt into a bowl. Beat the butter and sugar in a bowl with an electric mixer on medium-high speed until pale and creamy. Add the mint extract and egg, beating until just blended.

With the mixer on low speed, gradually beat in the flour mixture. Press the dough into a disk, wrap in plastic wrap (cling film), and chill in the refrigerator for 30 minutes.

Preheat the oven to 350°F (180°C/gas 4). Line two large baking sheets with parchment paper.

Roll out the dough on a lightly floured work surface to ⅛ inch (3 mm) thick. Use a 2-inch (5-cm) cookie cutter to cut out the cookies. Gather the dough scraps, re-roll, and continue cutting out cookies until all the dough is used. Transfer the cookies to the prepared baking sheets, placing them 1 inch (2.5 cm) apart.

Bake for 6–8 minutes, until just golden at the edges. Rotate the baking sheets halfway through for even baking.

Let the cookies cool on the baking sheets for 2–3 minutes, until they are firm enough to move. Transfer to a wire rack and let cool completely.

Filling: Bring the cream to a boil in a small saucepan over low heat. Remove from the heat and stir in the white chocolate and mint extract until smooth. Cool until firm but not set, about 30 minutes. Sandwich the cookies together in pairs with the filling.

Glaze: Melt the chocolate and butter in a double boiler over barely simmering water. Spread on the cookies. Chill until set, about 30 minutes.

. . .

If you liked this recipe, you will love these as well.

CHOCOLATE RICOTTA SANDWICHES

CHOCOLATE MOUSSE SANDWICHES

MERINGUES WITH CHOCOLATE RICOTTA CREAM

Makes: 12–15 filled
    cookies
Preparation: 30 minutes
    + 45 minutes to rest
Cooking: 15–20 minutes
Level: 3

. . . . .

Macaroons are made with a mixture of egg whites, ground nuts (usually almonds), and sugar. Crisp and meringue-like in texture, they make a delicate dessert.

CHOCOLATE MACAROONS

Macaroons

1	cup (150 g) confectioners' (icing) sugar
1	tablespoon unsweetened cocoa powder
1	cup (100 g) ground almonds
2	large egg whites

Filling

3	ounces (90 g) dark chocolate, coarsely chopped
1	tablespoon skimmed milk, warmed a little

Macaroons: Line three large baking sheets with edible rice paper. Sift the confectioners' sugar and cocoa into a bowl. Stir in the almonds.

Beat the egg whites in a medium bowl with an electric mixer on medium speed until stiff and dry. Add half the almond and cocoa mixture to the meringue and use a large metal spoon to fold it in. Fold in the remaining almond and cocoa mixture.

Transfer to a piping bag and pipe out 24–30 circles about 1½ inches (3–4 cm) in diameter on the baking sheets, spacing about 1 inch (2.5 cm) apart.

Put the baking sheets in a cool dry place and let rest for 30 minutes. The macaroons should harden slightly and will not stick to your finger if you poke them gently.

Preheat the oven to 350°F (180°C/gas 4). Bake the macaroons for 15–20 minutes, until risen and smooth on top. If they begin to split, crack the oven door open a fraction to cool it down slightly.

Remove from the oven and let the macaroons cool completely on the baking sheets.

Filling: Melt the chocolate in a double boiler over barely simmering water, or in the microwave. Stir in the warm milk until smooth. Leave to cool and thicken, about 15 minutes. Sandwich the macaroons together in pairs, and serve.

. . .

If you liked this recipe, you will love these as well.

CHUNKY CHOCOLATE
MACAROONS

MERINGUES WITH
CHOCOLATE RICOTTA
CREAM

DOUBLE CHOCOLATE
MERINGUES

Makes: 16–18 filled
    cookies
Preparation: 20 minutes
    + 2 hours to cool
Cooking: 15–20 minutes
Level: 2

. . . . .

Use a food processor to grind the almonds yourself for these macaroons. You want them quite finely ground but still with a little bit of texture.

CHUNKY CHOCOLATE MACAROONS

Macaroons

2	large egg whites
1	cup (200 g) sugar
6	tablespoons unsweetened cocoa powder, sifted
2	cups (200 g) almost finely ground almonds

Filling

4	ounces (120 g) dark chocolate, melted
$1/2$	teaspoon almond oil

Macaroons: Preheat the oven to 325°F (170°C/gas 3). Line two large baking sheets with edible rice paper.

Beat the egg whites in a large bowl with an electric mixer on medium speed until soft peaks form. Gradually add the sugar, beating until stiff, glossy peaks form.

Fold in the cocoa and almonds until completely blended. The batter should be quite thick and sticky.

Wet your hands and shape 1 heaped teaspoon of dough into a ball. Pinch the ball with your fingers to form a teardrop shape and place on one of the prepared baking sheets. Repeat until all the dough is used, spacing the cookies about 1 inch (2.5 cm) apart.

Bake for 15–20 minutes, until firm and slightly cracked on top. Rotate the baking sheets halfway through for even baking.

Transfer the cookies still on the rice paper to a wire rack and let cool completely, about 1 hour.

Filling: Melt the chocolate in a double boiler over barely simmering water, or in the microwave. Let cool a little, then stir in the oil.

Spoon about 1 teaspoon of filling onto half the cookies. Cover with the remaining cookies. Press together gently so the chocolate oozes out slightly. Return to the rack and let harden before serving, about 1 hour.

. . .

If you liked this recipe, you will love these as well.

CHOCOLATE RICOTTA
SANDWICHES

CHOCOLATE MACAROONS

DOUBLE CHOCOLATE
MERINGUES

MERINGUES
with chocolate ricotta cream

Meringues

2	large egg whites
1/4	teaspoon vanilla extract (essence)
1/2	cup (100 g) superfine (caster) sugar

Chocolate Ricotta Filling

1/2	cup (120 g) fresh ricotta cheese, drained
1	ounce (30 g) dark chocolate, grated
1	tablespoon heavy (double) cream

Meringues: Preheat the oven to 250°F (130°C/gas 1/2). Line two large baking sheets with parchment paper.

Beat the egg whites in a bowl with an electric mixer on medium speed until soft peaks form. Beat in the vanilla and then gradually add the sugar, beating until stiff, glossy peaks form. Place teaspoonfuls of the mixture onto the prepared baking sheets, then spread into disks about 1 inch (2.5 cm) in diameter.

Bake for about 1 hour, until crisp and dry. Rotate the baking sheets halfway through for even baking. Transfer the cookies still on the parchment paper to a wire rack and let cool completely, about 1 hour.

Chocolate Ricotta Filling: Beat the ricotta, chocolate, and cream in a bowl until well combined. Spread half the meringues with the filling. Cover with the remaining meringues, and serve.

Makes: 15–20 filled cookies Preparation: 20 minutes + 1 hour to cool Cooking: 1 hour Level: 2

DOUBLE CHOCOLATE MERINGUES

Meringues

4	large egg whites
1/4	teaspoon cream of tartar
1	cup (200 g) superfine (caster) sugar
2	tablespoons unsweetened cocoa powder
1	cup (100 g) finely ground almonds
1	teaspoon almond extract (essence)

Filling

3 1/2	ounces (100 g) dark chocolate, finely chopped

Meringues: Preheat the oven to 325°F (170°C/gas 3). Line three large baking sheets with parchment paper.

Beat the egg whites and cream of tartar in a bowl with an electric mixer on medium speed until soft peaks form. Add the sugar, beating until stiff, glossy peaks form. Fold in the cocoa, almonds, and almond extract.

Spoon the mixture into a pastry (piping) bag with a 1/2-inch (1-cm) nozzle. Pipe sixty 1-inch (2.5-cm) meringues onto the prepared baking sheets, spacing 1 inch (2.5 cm) apart.

Bake for 15 minutes, until crisp and dry. Rotate the baking sheets halfway through for even baking. Transfer the cookies still on the parchment paper to a wire rack and let cool completely.

Filling: Melt the chocolate in a double boiler over barely simmering water. Let cool a little. Dip the bases of half the meringues into the chocolate and sandwich together.

Makes: 30 filled cookies Preparation: 30 minutes Cooking: 15 minutes Level: 2

Meringues are a classic cookie and dessert with a long history. The earliest recipe for meringues appears in a French cook book first published in 1692.

Light and airy, meringues are a delicious treat with tea or coffee. If you are following a low-fat diet, dry meringues (no cream fillings!), contain almost no fat and can be served as an occasional treat.

Makes: 6
Preparation: 30 minutes
+ 1 hour to cool
Cooking: 1 hour
Level: 2

. . . . .

Serve these meringues for dessert. Fill with the berries and cream just before bringing to the table so that they don't become soggy and unappetizing.

CHOCOLATE MERINGUES
with berries & cream

Meringues

3 large egg whites

1 cup (200 g) superfine (caster) sugar

2 tablespoons unsweetened cocoa powder

2 ounces (60 g) dark chocolate, finely grated

Berries & Cream

1 cup (150 g) strawberries, hulled, quartered

1 cup (150 g) blueberries

1 tablespoon superfine (caster) sugar

1 cup (250 ml) heavy (double) cream

1/2 teaspoon vanilla extract (essence)

Grated dark chocolate, extra, to serve

Meringues: Preheat the oven to 250°F (130°C/gas 1/2). Line two large baking sheets with parchment paper. Draw six 4-inch (10-cm) circles on the parchment paper. Turn the paper over, pencil-side down.

Beat the egg whites in a bowl with an electric mixer on medium speed until soft peaks form. Add the sugar, 1 tablespoon at a time, beating well after each addition. Continue beating until the meringue is thick and glossy. Sift the cocoa over the meringue. Add the grated chocolate. Using a large metal spoon, gently fold in until just combined.

Using the circles as a guide, spoon the meringue onto the baking sheets. Make a small indentation in the center of each meringue. Bake for 1 hour.

Turn off the oven off. Leave the meringues to cool in the oven with the door ajar for 1 hour. Transfer to a wire rack and let cool completely.

Berries & Cream: Combine the strawberries and blueberries in a bowl. Sprinkle with the sugar, stirring to combine. Set aside for 15 minutes.

Beat the cream and vanilla until soft peaks form.

Place the meringues on serving plates. Top with the cream and berries. Sprinkle with the chocolate, and serve.

. . .

If you liked this recipe, you will love these as well.

CHOCOLATE MACAROONS

MERINGUES WITH CHOCOLATE RICOTTA CREAM

DOUBLE CHOCOLATE MERINGUES

bars & brownies

Here you will find 21 delicious recipes.
Try our simple No-bake chocolate squares
and Chocolate walnut brownies, or the
richer Chocolate caramel squares and
Chocolate panforte.

Makes: 12 squares

Preparation: 15 minutes
+ 2 hours to chill

Cooking: 5 minutes

Level: 1

. . . . .

Children will love this old favorite, and they will also enjoy helping to prepare it.

NO-BAKE CHOCOLATE SQUARES

Base

1   cup (250 g) salted butter

4   tablespoons unsweetened cocoa powder

1   tablespoon firmly packed light brown sugar

2   tablespoons light corn (golden) syrup

2   cups (250 g) crushed graham cracker or digestive biscuit crumbs

Frosting

4   ounces (120 g) dark chocolate, coarsely chopped

Base: Butter an 8-inch (20-cm) square baking pan. Line with parchment paper or aluminum foil, leaving a 2-inch (5-cm) overhang on two sides.

Melt the butter in a small saucepan over low heat. Stir in the cocoa, brown sugar, and corn syrup. Bring to a boil and let simmer for 1 minute. Remove from the heat and stir in the cookie crumbs.

Spoon the mixture into the prepared pan, pressing down firmly with the back of a spoon to create an even layer.

Frosting: Melt the chocolate in a double boiler over barely simmering water, or in the microwave. Pour the melted chocolate over the base. Chill in the refrigerator until set, at least 2 hours.

Lift the brownie carefully onto a board using the overhanging paper or foil. Cut into squares and serve.

. . .

If you liked this recipe, you will love these as well.

RUM & RAISIN BROWNIES

CHOCOLATE MACADAMIA BROWNIES

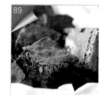

CAPPUCCINO BROWNIES

CHOCOLATE CHIP WEDGES

2¼ cups (330 g) all-purpose (plain) flour
1 teaspoon baking soda (bicarbonate of soda)
½ teaspoon salt
1 cup (250 g) unsalted butter, softened
¾ cup (150 g) sugar
¾ cup (150 g) firmly packed light brown sugar
½ teaspoon vanilla extract (essence)
2 large eggs, lightly beaten
1 cup (180 g) dark chocolate chips

Preheat the oven to 375°F (190°C/gas 5). Set out a 14-inch (35-cm) pizza pan.

Sift the flour, baking soda, and salt into a bowl. Beat the butter and both sugars in a bowl with an electric mixer on medium-high speed until creamy. Add the vanilla and eggs, beating until just blended.

With the mixer on low speed, gradually beat in the flour mixture and chocolate chips. Spread the mixture evenly in the prepared pan.

Bake for 15–20 minutes, until lightly browned. Let cool completely in the pan. Cut into 20 wedges and serve.

Makes: 20 wedges Preparation: 10 minutes Cooking: 15–20 minutes Level: 1

BROWN SUGAR BROWNIES
with chocolate & nuts

1 cup (150 g) all-purpose (plain) flour
¼ teaspoon baking soda (bicarbonate of soda)
½ cup (120 g) salted butter
1¼ cups (250 g) firmly packed dark brown sugar
2 large eggs
1 teaspoon vanilla extract (essence)
½ cup (60 g) salted roasteds peanuts, divided
½ cup (90 g) dark chocolate chips

Preheat the oven to 350°F (180°C/gas 4). Butter and flour an 8-inch (20-cm) square baking pan. Sift the flour and baking soda into a bowl.

Melt the butter in a medium saucepan over low heat. Remove from the heat. Add the brown sugar and whisk until smooth. Cool the mixture for 5 minutes, then whisk in the eggs and vanilla.

Stir in the flour mixture followed by half of the peanuts and half the chocolate chips. Spread the batter evenly in the prepared pan. Sprinkle with the remaining peanuts and chocolate chips.

Bake for 30–35 minutes, until golden brown and a toothpick inserted into the center comes out clean. Cool in the pan on a wire rack for a few minutes.

Serve warm straight from the pan.

Makes: 12 brownies Preparation: 20 minutes Cooking: 30–35 minutes Level: 1

These chocolate chip wedges fall somewhere between a cookie and a brownie. If you like a crisper, more cookie-like texture, bake for a few minutes longer.

The salt in the peanuts adds a delicious note to the crunchy topping on this rich brownie.

Makes: 12–16 squares
Preparation: 30 minutes
  + 4 hours to soak
Cooking: 40–45 minutes
Level: 1

. . . . .

Rum and raisin is a classic combination. If liked, you can reinforce the rum flavor by drizzling the finished brownies with 1–2 tablespoons of dark rum just before cutting into squares to serve.

RUM & RAISIN BROWNIES

1	cup (170 g) raisins
1/2	cup (120 ml) dark rum
1/2	cup (120 g) salted butter, chopped
10	ounces (300 g) dark chocolate, finely chopped
3/4	cup (150 g) firmly packed dark brown sugar
2	large eggs, lightly beaten
1 1/2	cups (225 g) all-purpose (plain) flour
1	cup (120 g) walnuts, coarsely chopped
1/4	cup (60 ml) sour cream

Combine the raisins and rum in a medium saucepan over low heat. Cook, stirring occasionally, for 2 minutes, until just heated through. Remove from the heat. Cover with plastic wrap (cling film) and set aside for 4 hours to soak.

Preheat the oven to 350°F (180°C/gas 4). Grease an 8-inch (20-cm) square pan. Line with parchment paper or aluminum foil, leaving a 2-inch (5-cm) overhang on two sides.

Combine the butter and chocolate in a heavy-based saucepan over low heat. Cook, stirring constantly, until the chocolate is melted and smooth. Remove from the heat and set aside to cool for a few minutes.

Add the brown sugar and eggs, stirring until well combined. Stir in the flour, followed by the raisin mixture, walnuts, and sour cream. Spoon into the prepared pan and smooth the surface.

Bake for 40–45 minutes, until a toothpick inserted into the center comes out with just a few moist crumbs attached.

Let cool on a wire rack for 30 minutes.

Lift the brownies carefully onto a board using the overhanging paper or foil. Let cool completely. Cut into squares to serve.

. . .

If you liked this recipe, you will love these as well.

NO-BAKE CHOCOLATE SQUARES

CHOCOLATE MACADAMIA BROWNIES

CHOCOLATE WALNUT BROWNIES

Makes: 12 brownies
Preparation: 20 minutes
    + 15 minutes to cool
Cooking: 50 minutes
Level: 1

CHOCOLATE MACADAMIA BROWNIES

8   ounces (250 g) dark chocolate, chopped

1   cup (250 g) salted butter, cut up

1½ cups (300 g) firmly packed light brown sugar

4   large eggs, lightly beaten

⅓   cup (50 g) unsweetened cocoa powder

1⅓ cups (200 g) all-purpose (plain) flour

1   teaspoon baking powder

½   cup (90 g) dark chocolate chips

½   cup (90 g) white chocolate chips

1   cup (120 g) salted macadamias, chopped

Preheat the oven to 325°F (170°C/gas 3). Lightly grease a 9-inch (23-cm) square baking pan. Line with parchment paper or aluminum foil, leaving a 2-inch (5-cm) overhang on two sides.

Melt the dark chocolate with the butter in a heavy-based saucepan over very low heat, stirring until smooth.

Whisk the brown sugar and eggs in a bowl until well combined. Stir in the chocolate mixture, followed by the cocoa, flour, baking powder, both chocolate chips, and the nuts.

Spoon the batter into the prepared pan, smoothing the top.

Bake for about 50 minutes, until a toothpick inserted into the center comes out with just a few moist crumbs attached.

Leave in the pan for 15 minutes. Lift the brownies carefully onto a board using the overhanging paper or foil. Cut into squares while still warm. Serve warm or at room temperature.

. . .

*If you liked this recipe,
you will love these as well.*

MACADAMIA BLONDIES

CHOCOLATE WALNUT
BROWNIES

CHOCOLATE PANFORTE

Makes: 12 blondies
Preparation: 20 minutes
    + 30 minutes to cool
Cooking: 50 minutes
Level: 1

MACADAMIA BLONDIES

14   ounces (400 g)
        white chocolate,
        grated

2/3   cup (150 g) unsalted
        butter

3   large eggs, lightly
        beaten

1   cup (150 g) all-
        purpose (plain) flour

1/2   cup (60 g) whole
        milk powder

1/4   cup (50 g) superfine
        (caster) sugar

1/4   teaspoon baking
        powder

1   cup (150 g) whole
        macadamia nuts

Preheat the oven to 350°F (180°C/gas 4). Grease an 8-inch (20-cm) square pan. Line with parchment paper or aluminum foil, leaving a 2-inch (5-cm) overhang on two sides.

Combine 6 ounces (180 g) of the white chocolate with the butter in a heavy-based saucepan over very low heat. Stir until the chocolate and butter are melted and well combined. Set aside to cool a little.

Add the eggs and stir with a wooden spoon until well combined.

Combine the flour, milk powder, sugar, and baking powder in a medium bowl. Stir in the remaining white chocolate and the macadamia nuts. Add the butter mixture and stir until just combined. Spoon the batter into the prepared pan, smoothing the top with the spoon.

Bake for about 50 minutes, until a toothpick inserted into the center comes out with just a few moist crumbs attached. Rotate the pan halfway through for even baking.

Leave in the pan for 30 minutes. Lift the blondies carefully onto a board using the overhanging paper or foil. Cut into squares while still warm. Let cool completely before serving.

. . .

If you liked this recipe, you will love these as well.

WHITE CHOCOLATE MACADAMIA COOKIES

CHOCOLATE MACADAMIA BROWNIES

ALMOND & NUTELLA SQUARES

Makes: 12 brownies
Preparation: 20 minutes
    + 15 minutes to cool
Cooking: 30–35 minutes
Level: 1

CINNAMON FUDGE BROWNIES

Brownies

$^1/_2$	cup (75 g) all-purpose (plain) flour
$1^1/_2$	teaspoons ground cinnamon
6	ounces (180 g) dark chocolate, chopped
$^3/_4$	cup (180 g) salted butter
4	large eggs
1	cup (200 g) sugar
$1^1/_2$	teaspoons vanilla extract (essence)
1	cup (120 g) coarsely chopped walnuts

Dark Chocolate Ganache

6	ounces (180 g) dark chocolate, chopped
3	tablespoons unsalted butter
2	tablespoons heavy (double) cream

Brownies: Preheat the oven to 350°F (180°C/gas 4). Butter an 8-inch (20-cm) square baking pan. Line with parchment paper or aluminum foil, leaving a 2-inch (5-cm) overhang on two sides.

Sift the flour and cinnamon into a small bowl. Melt the chocolate and butter in a double boiler over barely simmering water. Turn off the heat and let stand over the water.

Beat the eggs and sugar in large bowl with an electric mixer on medium-high speed until thick and pale. Beat in the vanilla. Fold in the flour mixture. Gradually add the chocolate to the egg mixture, beating until just combined. Stir in the walnuts. Pour into the prepared pan, smoothing the top with a spoon.

Bake for 30–35 minutes, until the top is set and a toothpick inserted into the center comes out with just a few moist crumbs attached.

Leave in the pan for 15 minutes. Lift the brownies carefully onto a board using the overhanging paper or foil.

Dark Chocolate Ganache: Stir the chocolate, butter, and cream in a heavy-based saucepan over low heat until smooth.

Pour evenly over the brownies, letting it run down the sides. Cut into squares and serve.

. . .

If you liked this recipe, you will love these as well.

CHOCOLATE BARS
WITH WALNUT &
MARSHMALLOW TOPPING

AZTEC BROWNIES

GINGER FUDGE
BROWNIES

Makes: 12–16 brownies
Preparation: 20 minutes
+ 3 hours to cool
& chill
Cooking: 30–35 minutes
Level: 1

CAPPUCCINO BROWNIES

Brownies

$1/2$	cup (120 g) salted butter, diced
3	ounces (90 g) dark chocolate, chopped
$1^1/2$	cups (300 g) sugar
3	large eggs
$3/4$	cup (120 g) all-purpose (plain) flour
1	tablespoon instant espresso powder
$1^1/2$	teaspoons vanilla extract (essence)

White Chocolate Ganache

6	ounces (180 g) white chocolate, chopped
5	tablespoons (75 ml) heavy (double) cream
$1/4$	teaspoon ground cinnamon

Brownies: Preheat the oven to 325°F (170°C/gas 3). Butter an 8-inch (20-cm) square baking pan. Line with parchment paper or aluminum foil, leaving a 2-inch (5-cm) overhang on two sides.

Melt the butter and chocolate in a double boiler over barely simmering water. Remove from the heat and beat in the sugar. Whisk in the eggs one at a time, followed by the flour, coffee, and vanilla. Pour into the prepared pan, smoothing the surface with a spoon.

Bake for 30–35 minutes, until the top is set and a toothpick inserted into the center comes out with just a few moist crumbs attached. Cool in the pan on a wire rack for 1 hour.

White Chocolate Ganache: Whisk the white chocolate, cream, and cinnamon in a heavy-based saucepan over low heat until smooth. Pour evenly over the brownies in the pan.

Chill until the ganache is set, at least 2 hours. Lift the brownies carefully onto a board using the overhanging paper or foil. Cut into squares, and serve.

. . .

If you liked this recipe, you will love these as well.

CINNAMON FUDGE BROWNIES

MARBLED FUDGE BROWNIES

CHOCOLATE CHEESECAKE BARS

Makes: 16 squares
Preparation: 15 minutes
 + 30 minutes to cool
Cooking: 20–25 minutes
Level: 1

CHOCOLATE WALNUT BROWNIES

2/3 cup (150 g) salted butter

1 1/4 cups (250 g) sugar

1 cup (150 g) unsweetened cocoa powder + extra, to dust

2 teaspoons water

1 teaspoon vanilla extract (essence)

2 large eggs, chilled

1/3 cup (50 g) all-purpose (plain) flour

1 cup (120 g) walnut pieces

Preheat the oven to 350°F (180°C/gas 4). Butter an 8-inch (20-cm) square baking pan. Line with parchment paper or aluminum foil, leaving a 2-inch (5-cm) overhang on two sides.

Melt the butter in a medium saucepan over medium-low heat. Simmer until the butter stops foaming, stirring often, about 5 minutes. Remove from the heat and add the sugar, cocoa, water, and vanilla. Stir to blend. Let cool for 5 minutes.

Add the eggs to the warm mixture one at a time, beating until just combined after each addition. When the mixture looks thick and shiny, add the flour and stir until blended. Beat vigorously for 1 minute. Stir in the walnuts. Spoon the batter into the prepared pan, smoothing the surface.

Bake for 20–25 minutes, until a toothpick inserted into the center comes out with just a few moist crumbs attached.

Leave in the pan for 30 minutes. Lift the brownies carefully onto a board using the overhanging paper or foil. Dust with cocoa, cut into squares, and serve.

. . .

If you liked this recipe, you will love these as well.

78
BROWN SUGAR
BROWNIES WITH
CHOCOLATE & NUTS

82
CHOCOLATE MACADAMIA
BROWNIES

92
CHOCOLATE BARS
WITH WALNUT &
MARSHMALLOW TOPPING

Makes: 12–16 bars
Preparation: 20 minutes
    + 1 hour to chill
Cooking: 28–35 minutes
Level: 1

. . . . .

The mixed marshmallow, walnut, and chocolate topping makes these bars very rich and special.

CHOCOLATE BARS
with walnut & marshmallow topping

½ cup (120 g) salted butter

½ cup (75 g) unsweetened cocoa powder

1 cup (200 g) firmly packed light brown sugar

1 large egg, lightly beaten

½ cup (75 g) all-purpose (plain) flour

½ cup (120 ml) milk

1 teaspoon vanilla extract (essence)

1 cup (120 g) coarsely chopped marshmallows

1 cup (120 g) coarsely chopped walnuts

1 cup (180 g) dark chocolate chips

Preheat the oven to 350°F (180°C/gas 4). Butter an 8-inch (20-cm) square pan. Line with parchment paper or aluminum foil, leaving a 2-inch (5-cm) overhang on two sides.

Combine the butter and cocoa in a heavy-based saucepan over low heat, stirring constantly, until the butter has melted and the mixture is smooth. Remove from the heat and stir in the brown sugar, egg, flour, milk, and vanilla until well combined. Spread the mixture evenly in the prepared pan, smoothing the top.

Bake for 25–30 minutes, until a toothpick inserted into the center comes out clean.

Sprinkle evenly with the marshmallows, walnuts, and chocolate chips. Return to the oven and bake for 3–5 more minutes, until the marshmallows puff up.

Cool in the pan to room temperature on a wire rack, then chill until the topping hardens, about 1 hour.

Lift the cake carefully onto a board using the overhanging paper or foil. Cut into 12–16 bars, and serve.

. . .

If you liked this recipe, you will love these as well.

CHOCOLATE CHIP WEDGES

BROWN SUGAR BROWNIES WITH CHOCOLATE & NUTS

CHOCOLATE PANFORTE

Makes: 12 squares
Preparation: 15 minutes
    + 1 hour to cool
Cooking: 25–30 minutes
Level: 1

. . . . .

The ancient Aztecs were among the first people to consume chocolate. They made a chocolate drink, laced with chilies. Our brownies are inspired by this age-old chocolate-chili combo.

AZTEC BROWNIES

12	ounces (350 g) dark chocolate, finely grated
1/2	cup (120 g) butter, chopped
1/3	cup (70 g) sugar
2	large eggs, beaten lightly
1	cup (150 g) all-purpose (plain) flour
1	teaspoon hot chili powder
1/2	cup (90 g) dark chocolate chips
	Unsweetened cocoa powder, to dust

Preheat the oven to 350°F (180°C/gas 4). Grease an 8-inch (20-cm) square pan with butter. Line with parchment paper or aluminum foil, leaving a 2-inch (5-cm) overhang on two sides.

Combine the finely grated chocolate and butter in a heavy-based saucepan over very low heat. Use a metal spoon to stir until melted. Add the sugar and cook, stirring constantly, for 2 more minutes. Remove from the heat and let cool for 5 minutes.

Add the eggs, flour, and chili powder, stirring until well combined. Add the chocolate chips, stirring until just combined. Spoon into prepared pan, smoothing the surface.

Bake for 25–30 minutes, until a toothpick inserted into the center comes out with just a few moist crumbs attached.

Leave in the pan on a wire rack for 1 hour.

Lift the brownies carefully onto a board using the overhanging paper or foil. Dust with cocoa, cut into 12 squares, and serve.

. . .

If you liked this recipe, you will love these as well.

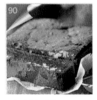

CHOCOLATE WALNUT BROWNIES

CHOCOLATE PANFORTE

CHURROS WITH AZTEC SAUCE

Makes: 16 squares
Preparation: 25 minutes
    + 1 hour to cool
Cooking: 50–60 minutes
Level: 1

MARBLED FUDGE BROWNIES

Chocolate Batter

1	cup (150 g) all-purpose (plain) flour
1/4	cup (30 g) unsweetened cocoa powder
1/2	teaspoon baking powder
1/2	teaspoon salt
8	ounces (250 g) dark chocolate, coarsely chopped
1/2	cup (120 g) unsalted butter
1 1/4	cups (250 g) sugar
3	large eggs

Cream Cheese Batter

4	ounces (120 g) cream cheese, softened
2	tablespoons unsalted butter, softened
1/4	cup (50 g) sugar
1	large egg
2	tablespoons all-purpose (plain) flour

Preheat the oven to 350°F (180°C/gas 4). Grease a 9-inch (23-cm) square baking pan. Line with parchment paper or aluminum foil, leaving a 2-inch (5-cm) overhang on two sides.

Chocolate Batter: Sift the flour, cocoa, baking powder, and salt into a bowl.

Melt the chocolate and butter in a double boiler over barely simmering water. Remove from the heat and beat in the sugar. Add the eggs one at a time, beating until just combined after each addition. Gradually add the flour mixture, mixing until just combined.

Cream Cheese Batter: Beat the cream cheese and butter in a bowl until smooth. Beat in the sugar, egg, and flour.

Place alternate spoonfuls of the chocolate and cream-cheese batters in the prepared pan. Swirl with a knife to create a marbled pattern.

Bake for 50–60 minutes, until a toothpick inserted into the center comes out with just a few moist crumbs attached.

Leave in the pan for 1 hour. Lift the brownies carefully onto a board using the overhanging paper or foil. Transfer to a rack and let cool completely. Cut into squares and serve.

. . .

If you liked this recipe, you will love these as well.

CHOCOLATE SWIRL CUPCAKES

QUICK MARBLE CAKE

MARBLED CHEESECAKE

Makes: 16 brownies
Preparation: 15 minutes
  + 15 minutes to cool
Cooking: 30–35 minutes
Level: 1

GINGER FUDGE BROWNIES

- ½ cup (120 g) unsalted butter
- 3½ ounces (100 g) bittersweet chocolate, coarsely chopped
- 1 cup (200 g) sugar
- ⅔ cup (100 g) all-purpose (plain) flour
- ¼ cup (30 g) unsweetened cocoa powder
- 2 large eggs
- 1 teaspoon finely grated fresh ginger
- ½ teaspoon vanilla extract (essence)
- ½ teaspoon ground nutmeg
- ½ teaspoon ground ginger
- ¼ teaspoon salt
- ⅛ teaspoon ground cloves

Preheat the oven to 325°F (160°C/gas 3). Butter an 8-inch (20-cm) square baking dish. Line with parchment paper or aluminum foil, leaving a 2-inch (5-cm) overhang on two sides.

Melt the butter and chocolate in a double boiler over barely simmering water until smooth. Remove from the heat and stir in all the remaining ingredients. Spoon the batter into the prepared pan, smoothing the top.

Bake for 30–35 minutes, until a toothpick inserted into the center comes out with just a few moist crumbs attached.

Let cool in the pan on a wire rack for 15 minutes.

Lift the brownies carefully onto a board using the overhanging paper or foil. Return to the wire a rack and let cool completely. Cut into 16 squares, and serve.

. . .

If you liked this recipe, you will love these as well.

CINNAMON FUDGE BROWNIES

AZTEC BROWNIES

COCONUT FUDGE BROWNIES

Makes: 12–16 squares
Preparation: 20 minutes
   + time to cool
Cooking: 35–42 minutes
Level: 1

. . . . .

These almond squares are spread with delicious Nutella, an Italian chocolate almond spread that has become famous around the world. If you are fond of Nutella, add a little extra to the topping.

ALMOND & NUTELLA SQUARES

Base

1/2	cup (120 g) salted butter, softened
1/3	cup (50 g) confectioners' (icing) sugar
1	cup (150 g) all-purpose (plain) flour
1	tablespoon unsweetened shredded (desiccated) coconut

Filling

3/4	cup (180 g) Nutella (chocolate hazelnut spread)

Topping

4	large egg whites
1	cup (100 g) finely ground almonds
3/4	cup (150 g) superfine (caster) sugar
4	drops of almond extract (essence)
3/4	cup (75 g) flaked almonds

Base: Preheat the oven to 350°F (180°C/gas 4). Grease an 8-inch (20-cm) pan. Line with parchment paper or aluminum foil, leaving a 2-inch (5-cm) overhang on two sides.

Beat the butter and confectioners' sugar in a bowl with an electric mixer on medium-high speed until pale and creamy.

With the mixer on low speed, add the flour and coconut, beating until well combined. Press the mixture evenly into the base of the prepared pan, smoothing the surface with the back of a spoon.

Bake for 10–12 minutes, until pale golden brown. Let cool for 10 minutes in the pan on a wire rack.

Filling: Spread the Nutella evenly over the base.

Topping: Beat the egg whites in a large bowl with an electric mixer on medium speed until soft peaks form. Fold in the almonds, sugar, and almond extract. Spread over the filling, smoothing the surface. Sprinkle with the flaked almonds.

Bake for 25–30 minutes, until firm and golden brown. Rotate the pan halfway through for even baking.

Let cool completely in the pan. Lift the cake carefully onto a board using the overhanging paper or foil. Cut into squares and serve.

. . .

If you liked this recipe, you will love these as well.

CHUNKY CHOCOLATE MACAROONS

MACADAMIA BLONDIES

TWO-TONE BROWNIES

CHOCOLATE CHEESECAKE BARS

Base

8   ounces (250 g) dark chocolate, coarsely chopped

¼   cup (60 g) unsalted butter

½   cup (100 g) sugar

2   large eggs

⅔   cup (100 g) all-purpose (plain) flour

⅓   cup (50 g) finely ground almonds

½   teaspoon baking powder

⅛   teaspoon salt

⅓   teaspoon almond extract (essence)

Cheesecake

1   pound (500 g) cream cheese, softened

1   cup (250 ml) sweetened condensed milk

¼   cup (60 ml) sour cream

2   teaspoons vanilla extract (essence)

Frosting

4   ounces (120 g) dark chocolate, coarsely chopped

2   tablespoons unsalted butter

Base: Preheat the oven to 350°F (180°C/gas 4). Butter and flour an 8 x 12-inch (20 x 30-cm) baking pan. Line with parchment paper or aluminum foil, leaving a 2-inch (5-cm) overhang on two sides.

Place the chocolate, butter, and sugar in a double boiler over barely simmering water. Stir until melted and smooth.

Remove from the heat and beat in the eggs, flour, almonds, baking powder, salt, and almond extract. Spoon the batter into the prepared pan, smoothing the top with the back of the spoon.

Bake for about 30 minutes, until a toothpick inserted into the center comes out clean. Place the pan on a wire rack and let cool completely.

Cheesecake: Beat the cream cheese, condensed milk, sour cream, and vanilla with an electric mixer on low speed until smooth and creamy. Spread over the cooled cake in the pan. Chill in the refrigerator until set, at least 2 hours.

Frosting: Melt the chocolate and butter in a double boiler over barely simmering water. Let cool a little then spread evenly over the cheesecake layer. Chill for at least 30 minutes.

Lift the cake carefully onto a board using the overhanging paper or foil. Cut into bars, and serve.

. . .

If you liked this recipe, you will love these as well.

CHOCOLATE ORANGE SQUARES

CHOCOLATE CARAMEL SQUARES

CHOCOLATE MINT BARS

COCONUT FUDGE BROWNIES

2/3 cup (100 g) unsweetened cocoa powder

1 cup (250 g) salted butter

2 1/2 cups (500 g) superfine (caster) sugar

4 large eggs, beaten

2/3 cup (100 g) all-purpose (plain) flour

2/3 cup (100 g) unsweetened shredded (desiccated) coconut

Preheat the oven to 350°F (180°C/gas 4). Butter an 8-inch (20-cm) square pan. Line with parchment paper or aluminum foil, leaving a 2-inch (5-cm) overhang on two sides.

Combine the cocoa, butter, and sugar in a heavy-based saucepan over low heat and gently melt, stirring constantly to prevent the mixture from burning.

Set aside to cool slightly, then gradually stir in the eggs, followed by the flour and coconut. Spoon into the prepared pan.

Bake for 40–45 minutes, until dry on top and set around the edges.

Let cool completely in the pan on a wire rack. Lift carefully onto a board using the overhanging paper or foil. Cut into squares and serve.

Makes: 16 brownies Preparation: 15 minutes Cooking: 45–50 minutes Level: 1

TWO-TONE BROWNIES

Base

1 cup (150 g) all-purpose (plain) flour

4 tablespoons sugar

1/2 cup (120 g) butter

Topping

4 tablespoons self-rising flour

4 tablespoons cocoa

1 large egg

1 teaspoon vanilla extract (essence)

1 (14-ounce/400-ml) can sweetened condensed milk

7 ounces (200 g) milk chocolate, grated

2/3 cup (90 g) walnuts

Base: Preheat the oven to 350°F (180°C/gas 4). Grease a 9-inch (23-cm) square pan.

Combine the flour and sugar in a bowl. Cut in the butter until the mixture is crumbly. Press firmly into the prepared pan in an even layer.

Bake for 15 minutes, until firm and lightly golden. Set aside to cool.

Topping: Combine the flour and cocoa in a bowl. Add the egg, vanilla, and condensed milk and stir until well blended. Stir in the chocolate and walnuts. Spread the mixture over the cooled base.

Bake for 20–25 minutes, until the brownies begin to pull away from the sides of the pan and the top feels dry.

Let cool completely in the pan on a wire rack. Cut into squares and serve.

Makes: 16–20 brownies Preparation: 30 minutes Cooking: 35–40 minutes Level: 1

These are the perfect brownie for coconut lovers. Be sure not to overbake, so that they keep a slightly gooey texture.

These deluxe brownies have a crisp cookie base and a thick, gooey brownie layer on top.

CHOCOLATE ORANGE SQUARES

Base

1 cup (150 g) all-purpose (plain) flour
2 tablespoons unsweetened cocoa powder
¹/₄ teaspoon salt
1 cup (250 g) butter
¹/₃ cup (70 g) sugar
¹/₃ cup (50 g) confectioners' (icing) sugar

Filling

Finely grated zest of 1 unwaxed orange
¹/₂ cup (125 ml) freshly squeezed orange juice
¹/₂ cup (125 ml) water
¹/₃ cup (50 g) cornstarch (cornflour)
1 teaspoon freshly squeezed lemon juice
1 tablespoon salted butter
¹/₂ cup (160 g) orange marmalade

Glaze

3 tablespoons cream
1¹/₂ teaspoons corn syrup (golden syrup)
3¹/₂ ounces (100 g) dark chocolate, grated

Base: Preheat the oven to 325°F (170°C/gas 3). Grease an 8-inch (20-cm) square baking pan. Line with parchment paper or aluminum foil, leaving a 2-inch (5-cm) overhang on two sides.

Sift the flour, cocoa, and salt into a bowl. Beat the butter, sugar, and confectioners' sugar in a large bowl with an electric mixer on medium-high speed until pale and creamy.

With the mixer on low speed, beat in the flour mixture. Firmly press the mixture into the prepared pan in a smooth, even layer. Prick all over with a fork.

Bake until firm to the touch, 25–30 minutes. Let cool for 10 minutes.

Filling: Mix the orange zest and juice, water, cornstarch, and lemon juice in a small saucepan over medium heat. Bring to a boil and simmer, stirring constantly, until thickened, about 1 minute.

Remove from the heat and stir in the butter and marmalade. Pour the filling over the base in an even layer.

Bake for 5 minutes. Cool completely in the pan. Chill in the refrigerator until set, about 1 hour.

Glaze: Bring the cream to a boil with the corn syrup in a small saucepan. Remove from the heat and stir in the chocolate until melted and smooth. Spread over the filling in an even layer.

Chill for 30 minutes. Lift the cake carefully onto a board using the overhanging paper or foil. Cut into squares and serve.

. . .

If you liked this recipe, you will love these as well.

CHOCOLATE
CHEESECAKE BARS

CHOCOLATE CARAMEL
SQUARES

CHOCOLATE MINT BARS

CHOCOLATE CARAMEL SQUARES

Base

3/4	cup (180 g) unsalted butter
1/3	cup (70 g) sugar
1	vanilla pod, split and seeds scraped out
1 1/2	cups (225 g) all-purpose (plain) flour

Caramel

1	cup (250 g) unsalted butter
1	(14-ounce/400-g) can sweetened condensed milk
4	tablespoons light corn (golden) syrup
1	teaspoon salt

Topping

12	ounces (350 g) milk chocolate

Base: Preheat the oven to 350°F (180°C/gas 4). Grease an 8-inch (20-cm) square baking pan. Line with parchment paper or aluminum foil, leaving a 2-inch (5-cm) overhang on two sides.

Rub the butter, sugar, vanilla seeds, and flour together in a bowl to make a coarse dough. Press the dough firmly into the prepared pan and prick all over with a fork.

Bake for 5 minutes, then reduce the oven temperature to 300°F (150°C/gas 2). Bake for 35 minutes. Let cool in the pan.

Caramel: Combine the butter, condensed milk, syrup, and salt in a saucepan and bring to a boil. Simmer over very low heat for 10 minutes.

Pour the caramel mixture over the base. Chill until the caramel has cooled and hardened slightly, about 30 minutes.

Topping: Melt the chocolate in a double boiler over barely simmering water, or in the microwave. Set aside to cool a little.

Pour the topping over the caramel. Chill until the chocolate has set, about 30 minutes. Lift the cake carefully onto a board using the overhanging paper or foil. Cut into squares and serve.

. . .

*If you liked this recipe,
you will love these as well.*

ALMOND & NUTELLA
SQUARES

CHOCOLATE ORANGE
SQUARES

CHOCOLATE PANFORTE

Makes: 12–16 pieces
Preparation: 30 minutes
    + 2 hours to set
    & cool
Cooking: 25–30 minutes
Level: 2

• • • • •

Panforte is an Italian specialty, from Siena, in Tuscany. It is made every fall when the new season's nuts are harvested. This version is a rich chocolate variation on traditional panforte. It is perfect for Christmas and other fall and winter holiday celebrations.

CHOCOLATE PANFORTE

Panforte

- 2 tablespoons raisins
- 1/2 cup (60 g) walnuts, chopped
- 1/4 cup (30 g) almonds, chopped
- 1/4 cup (30 g) hazelnuts, chopped
- 1/4 cup (30 g) pine nuts
- 2/3 cup (150 g) mixed candied (glacé) peel, cut into small cubes
- 1/3 cup (50 g) unsweetened cocoa powder
- 4 ounces (120 g) dark chocolate, grated
- 1/2 teaspoon ground cinnamon
- 1/2 teaspoon ground nutmeg
- 1/2 teaspoon ground coriander
- 1/2 teaspoon freshly ground black pepper
- 1/4 cup (60 ml) honey, warmed
- 2 1/3 cups (350 g) all-purpose (plain) flour
- 1/4 teaspoon fennel seeds
- 1/2 cup (120 ml) warm water + extra, as needed

Glaze

- 8 ounces (250 g) dark chocolate, chopped

Panforte: Soak the raisins in a small bowl of warm water for 20 minutes. Drain well.

Preheat the oven to 325°F (170°C/gas 3). Butter and flour a 10-inch (25-cm) square pan. Line with parchment paper or aluminum foil, leaving a 2-inch (5-cm) overhang on two sides.

Mix the walnuts, almonds, hazelnuts, pine nuts, candied peel, raisins, cocoa, chocolate, cinnamon, nutmeg, coriander, and pepper in a large bowl. Stir in the honey, flour, fennel seeds, and enough warm water to make a stiff dough.

Spoon the dough into the prepared pan, pressing down firmly, and smoothing the top.

Bake for 25–30 minutes, until firm to the touch. Cool in the pan for 30 minutes. Turn out onto a rack and let cool completely.

Glaze: Melt the chocolate in a double boiler over barely simmering water, or in the microwave. Set aside to cool for 10 minutes. Spread over the cake.

Let set for at least 1 hour. Lift the cake carefully onto a board using the overhanging paper or foil. Cut into bars, and serve.

• • •

If you liked this recipe, you will love these as well.

BROWN SUGAR
BROWNIES WITH
CHOCOLATE & NUTS

CHOCOLATE WALNUT
BROWNIES

CHOCOLATE BARS
WITH WALNUT &
MARSHMALLOW TOPPING

. . . . .

You could leave the green food coloring out of the filling, but it does add a touch of color to the finished dish. Serve on St. Patrick's Day!

CHOCOLATE MINT BARS

Base

1/3 cup (50 g) all-purpose (plain) flour

1/2 teaspoon baking powder

1/4 cup (30 g) unsweetened cocoa powder

3 1/2 ounces (100 g) dark chocolate, chopped

1/4 cup (60 g) salted butter

2 large eggs

3/4 cup (150 g) sugar

Filling

8 ounces (250 g) white chocolate, chopped

1/2 cup (120 ml) double (heavy) cream

2 teaspoons peppermint extract (essence)

Green food coloring

Frosting

5 ounces (150 g) dark chocolate

1 tablespoons light corn (golden) syrup

1/4 cup (60 g) salted butter

Base: Preheat the oven to 350°F (180°C/gas 4). Grease a 9-inch (23-cm) square pan. Line with parchment paper or aluminum foil, leaving a 2-inch (5-cm) overhang on two sides.

Sift the flour, baking powder, and cocoa into a bowl.

Melt the chocolate and butter in a double boiler over barely simmering water. Let cool to room temperature.

Beat the eggs and sugar in a bowl with an electric mixer on medium-high speed until pale and thickened. Fold the chocolate mixture into the egg mixture. Fold in the flour mixture. Pour into the prepared pan.

Bake for 15–20 minutes, until the top is just set. Let cool completely in the pan on a wire rack.

Filling: Put the white chocolate in a heatproof bowl. Heat the cream until just simmering, then pour over the white chocolate. Leave for a minute, then gently stir until the chocolate is melted and smooth. Stir in the peppermint and enough food coloring to make a mint color.

Chill until thickened, about 15 minutes. Spread over the brownie, then chill for 45 minutes.

Frosting: Melt the dark chocolate, syrup, and butter in a double boiler over barely simmering water. Let cool a little, then spread over the filling. Chill for 1 hour.

Lift the cake carefully onto a board using the overhanging paper or foil. Cut into bars and serve.

. . .

If you liked this recipe, you will love these as well.

CHOCOLATE MINT
CREAMS

CHOCOLATE MINT
CUPCAKES

CHOCOLATE MINT
TRUFFLE CAKE

muffins & cupcakes

Try our Chocolate banana muffins for breakfast, or amaze your dinner party guests with the Chocolate swirl cupcakes or Chocolate butterfly cupcakes.

Makes: 12 muffins
Preparation: 20 minutes
  + 1 hour to cool
Cooking: 15–20 minutes
Level: 1

. . . . .

Exotic passion fruit, also known as granadillas, originally come from the subtropical areas of Brazil, Paraguay, and Argentina. They are now grown in many different parts of the world.

WHITE CHOCOLATE MUFFINS
with passion fruit

Muffins

2	cups (300 g) all-purpose (plain) flour
2	teaspoons baking powder
1/2	cup (100 g) sugar
3 1/2	ounces (100 g) white chocolate, grated
1/2	cup (120 g) salted butter, melted, cooled
1/3	cup (90 ml) milk
2	large eggs, lightly beaten
1/4	cup (60 ml) passion fruit pulp
1	teaspoon vanilla extract (essence)

Passion Fruit Frosting

1 1/3	cups (200 g) confectioners' (icing) sugar
2	teaspoons boiling water
1 1/2	tablespoons passion fruit pulp

Muffins: Preheat the oven to 400°F (200°C/gas 6). Grease a standard 12-cup muffin pan.

Combine the flour, baking powder, sugar, and chocolate in a bowl. Make a well in the center.

Beat the butter, milk, eggs, passion fruit pulp, and vanilla in another bowl. Pour into the flour mixture. Gently fold until just combined. Spoon the batter into the paper liners, filling each one two-thirds full.

Bake for 15–20 minutes, until a toothpick inserted into the centers comes out clean.

Let rest in the pan for 5 minutes. Turn out onto a wire rack and let cool completely, about 1 hour.

Passion Fruit Frosting: Stir the confectioners' sugar, water, and passion fruit pulp in a bowl until smooth.

Spoon the frosting over the muffins, letting it drizzle down the sides. Let set before serving.

. . .

If you liked this recipe, you will love these as well.

CHOCOLATE PEAR MUFFINS

CHOCOLATE BANANA MUFFINS

MINI CHOCOLATE MUD CAKES

· · · · ·

These striking muffins make an elegant dessert.
Be sure to choose small, tasty pears, such as Corelias.

CHOCOLATE PEAR MUFFINS

10	small ripe pears, peeled, stalks still attached
3	cups (750 ml) water
2	teaspoons vanilla bean paste
1½	cups (300 g) superfine (caster) sugar
2	tablespoons unsweetened cocoa powder + ¼ cup (30 g) extra
7	ounces (200 g) dark chocolate, finely chopped
¾	cup (180 g) salted butter, melted
1⅓	cups (200 g) all-purpose (plain) flour
1	teaspoon baking powder
2	large eggs, lightly beaten

Preheat the oven to 350°F (180°C/gas 4). Lightly grease ten standard muffin pans. Use a melon baller to scoop out the base and core from each pear.

Combine the water, vanilla bean paste, and half the sugar in a medium saucepan over low heat. Cook and stir until the sugar dissolves, about 5 minutes.

Bring to a boil. Add the pears and simmer gently, turning occasionally, until the pears are tender, about 10 minutes. Use a slotted spoon to transfer the pears to a plate to drain.

Whisk the 2 tablespoons of cocoa into the syrup. Simmer until it thickens slightly, 10–15 minutes.

Combine the chocolate and butter in a double boiler over barely simmering water, stirring until smooth. Remove from the heat.

Add the flour, baking powder, eggs, extra ¼ cup of cocoa, and remaining sugar to the chocolate mixture and stir until well combined.

Spoon the batter into the muffin cups. Gently press a pear into the center of each muffin.

Bake for 20 minutes, until a toothpick inserted into the centers comes out clean. Set aside for 15 minutes to cool.

Carefully remove from the pans and divide among serving plates. Drizzle with the chocolate syrup, and serve.

· · ·

If you liked this recipe, you will love these as well.

CHOCOLATE PEAR
JALOUSIE

CHOCOLATE PEAR
GALETTES

EASY CHOCOLATE TART
WITH PEARS

CHOCOLATE BANANA MUFFINS

2 cups (300 g) all-purpose (plain) flour

2 teaspoons baking powder

2/3 cup (150 g) salted butter, softened

3/4 cup (150 g) sugar

1 teaspoon vanilla extract (essence)

2 large eggs

2 bananas, mashed

7 ounces (200 g) dark chocolate, grated

1/4 cup (60 ml) milk

Chocolate ganache (see page 136)

White chocolate curls, to decorate

Preheat the oven to 350°F (180°C/gas 4). Line 16 standard muffin cups with paper liners. Sift the flour and baking powder into a bowl.

Beat the butter, sugar, and vanilla in a bowl with an electric mixer on medium-high speed until pale and creamy. Add the eggs one at a time, beating until just combined after each addition. With the mixer on low speed, beat in the bananas and chocolate, followed by the flour mixture and milk. Spoon the batter into the paper liners, filling each one two-thirds full.

Bake for 20–25 minutes, until a toothpick inserted into the centers comes out clean. Set aside to cool completely, about 1 hour.

Prepare the chocolate ganache and spread over the muffins. Decorate with the white chocolate curls, and serve.

Makes: 16 muffins Preparation: 15 minutes + 1 hour to cool Cooking: 20–25 minutes Level: 1

MINI CHOCOLATE MUD CAKES

1/2 cup (120 g) salted butter, chopped

3 1/2 ounces (100 g) dark chocolate, chopped

1/2 cup (120 ml) hot water

2 teaspoons instant coffee powder

1/4 cup (60 ml) coffee liqueur

1 cup (200 g) firmly packed brown sugar

1 cup (150 g) self-raising flour

2 tablespoons cocoa

1 large egg

Chocolate ganache (see page 136)

Chocolate curls

Preheat the oven to 325°F (170°C/gas 3). Line a standard 12-cup muffin pan with paper liners.

Combine the butter, chocolate, hot water, coffee powder, and coffee liqueur in a medium saucepan over low heat, stirring until smooth. Remove from the heat. Stir in the brown sugar. Let cool for 5 minutes.

Sift the flour and cocoa into a bowl. Beat into the chocolate mixture until combined. Add the egg and beat to combine. Spoon the batter into the paper liners, filling each one two-thirds full.

Bake for 20–25 minutes, until a toothpick inserted into the centers comes out clean. Set aside to cool completely, about 1 hour.

Prepare the chocolate ganache and spread over the mud cakes. Decorate with the chocolate curls, and serve.

Makes: 12 mud cakes Preparation: 15 minutes + 1 hour to cool Cooking: 20–25 minutes Level: 1

The banana adds a delicious moist texture to these muffins. Omit the chocolate ganache and white chocolate curls for a lighter muffin, more suitable for breakfast or brunch.

Mud cakes are believed to have been invented in Mississippi in the 1970s. Their deep, gooey texture is said to resemble the mud that lines the banks of the famous river.

Makes: 30–36 cupcakes

Preparation: 30 minutes
+ 1¾ hours to cool
& set

Cooking: 20–25 minutes

Level: 1

· · · · ·

This recipe makes a large batch of chocolate chip cupcakes. You can replace the dark chocolate chips with milk or white chocolate chips, if preferred.

CHOCOLATE CHIP CUPCAKES

Cupcakes

3⅓	cups (500 g) all-purpose (plain) flour
1½	tablespoons baking powder
¼	teaspoon salt
1	cup (250 g) unsalted butter, softened
1¾	cups (350 g) sugar
1	tablespoon vanilla extract (essence)
1	cup (250 ml) milk
5	large egg whites
2	cups (360 g) dark chocolate chips

Chocolate Frosting

¼	cup (60 ml) heavy (double) cream
8	ounces (250 g) dark chocolate, finely chopped
1	teaspoon vanilla extract (essence)
½	cup (90 g) dark chocolate chips

Cupcakes: Preheat the oven to 350°F (180°C/gas 4). Line three standard 12-cup muffin pans with paper liners.

Sift the flour, baking powder, and salt into a large bowl.

Beat the butter, sugar, and vanilla in a bowl with an electric mixer on medium-high speed until pale and creamy. With the mixer on low speed, gradually beat in the flour mixture, alternating with the milk.

Beat the egg whites in a separate bowl until stiff peaks form. Fold into the batter. Fold in the chocolate chips.

Spoon the batter into the paper liners, filling each one two-thirds full.

Bake for 20–25 minutes, until a toothpick inserted into the centers come out clean. Let cool in the pans for 5 minutes. Turn out onto wire racks and let cool completely, about 1 hour.

Chocolate Frosting: Bring the cream to a boil in a small saucepan over low heat. Add the chocolate. Simmer, stirring constantly, until the chocolate is melted and smooth. Remove from the heat and stir in the vanilla and chocolate chips. Let cool slightly, 10–15 minutes.

Spread over the cupcakes. Let set before serving, about 30 minutes.

· · ·

If you liked this recipe, you will love these as well.

CHOCOLATE BANANA MUFFINS

MINI CHOCOLATE MUD CAKES

RED VELVET CUPCAKES

Makes: 24 cupcakes

Preparation: 45 minutes
   + 1½ hours to cool
   & set

Cooking: 20–25 minutes

Level: 2

. . . . .

You will need two pastry (piping) bags to complete the decoration on these striking cupcakes.

RED VELVET CUPCAKES

Cupcakes

2⅓   cups (350 g) all-purpose (plain) flour
⅓   cup (50 g) unsweetened cocoa powder
1   teaspoon baking soda (bicarbonate of soda)
1   teaspoon salt
½   cup (120 g) unsalted butter, softened
1½   cups (300 g) sugar
4   large egg yolks
3   tablespoons red food coloring
1½   teaspoons vanilla extract (essence)
1   teaspoon white vinegar
1   cup (250 ml) buttermilk

Frosting

8   ounces (250 g) white chocolate
1   cup (250 g) salted butter
1½   cups (225 g) confectioners' (icing) sugar
1   teaspoon vanilla extract (essence)
2   tablespoons unsweetened cocoa powder

Cupcakes: Preheat the oven to 350°F (180°C/gas 4). Line two 12-cup muffin pans with paper liners.

Sift the flour, cocoa, baking soda, and salt into a bowl. Beat the butter and sugar in a bowl with an electric mixer on medium-high speed until pale and creamy. Add the egg yolks one at a time, beating until just combined after each addition. Add the red food coloring, vanilla, and vinegar, beating until just combined.

With the mixer on low speed, gradually beat in the flour mixture, alternating with the buttermilk.

Spoon the batter into the paper liners, filling each one two-thirds full.

Bake for 20–25 minutes, until a toothpick inserted into the centers come out clean. Let the cupcakes cool in the pans for 5 minutes. Turn out onto wire racks and let cool completely, about 1 hour.

Frosting: Melt the white chocolate in a double boiler over barely simmering water, or in the microwave. Set aside to cool for a few minutes.

Beat in the butter, confectioners' sugar, and vanilla until smooth and creamy. Divide evenly between two small bowls. Stir the cocoa into one bowl. Fill one pastry (piping) bag with dark frosting and a second pastry bag with white frosting.

Pipe alternate rosettes of frosting over the cupcakes. Let set before serving, about 30 minutes.

. . .

*If you liked this recipe,
you will love these as well.*

BLACK FOREST
CUPCAKES

CHOCOLATE BROWNIE
CUPCAKES

RED VELVET CAKE

Makes: 12 cupcakes
Preparation: 30 minutes
   + 1 hour to cool
Cooking: 20–25 minutes
Level: 1

. . . . .

The flavors in these cupcakes are inspired by the famous Black Forest Cake.

BLACK FOREST CUPCAKES

Cupcakes

- 3¹⁄₂ ounces (100 g) dark chocolate, coarsely chopped
- ¹⁄₃ cup (90 ml) light (single) cream
- 1 cup (150 g) all-purpose (plain) flour
- 2 tablespoons unsweetened cocoa powder
- 1 teaspoon baking powder
- ¹⁄₈ teaspoon salt
- ¹⁄₃ cup (90 g) unsalted butter, softened
- 1 cup (200 g) sugar
- 2 large eggs
- 2 tablespoons cherry brandy
- ¹⁄₂ cup (120 g) drained maraschino cherries, coarsely chopped + 12 extra, to decorate

Topping

- ²⁄₃ cup (150 ml) heavy (double) cream
- 2 tablespoons confectioners' (icing) sugar
- ¹⁄₂ tablespoon cherry brandy
- 2 ounces (60 g) dark chocolate, coarsely grated

  Unsweetened cocoa powder, to dust

Cupcakes: Preheat the oven to 350°F (180°C/gas 4). Line a standard 12-cup muffin pan with paper liners.

Melt the chocolate and cream in a double boiler over barely simmering water, stirring until smooth. Remove from the heat and let cool.

Sift the flour, cocoa, baking powder, and salt into a bowl. Beat the butter and sugar in a bowl with an electric mixer on medium-high speed until pale and creamy. Add the eggs one at a time, beating until just blended after each addition.

With the mixer on low speed, gradually beat in the flour mixture, chocolate mixture, cherry brandy, and chopped cherries. Spoon the batter into the paper liners, filling each one two-thirds full.

Bake for 20–25 minutes, until risen and firm to the touch. Transfer the muffin pan to a wire rack. Let the cupcakes cool in the pans for 5 minutes. Turn out onto wire racks and let cool completely, about 1 hour.

Topping: Beat the cream in a small bowl with an electric mixer until it begins to thicken. Gradually add the confectioners' sugar, beating until soft peaks form. Stir in the cherry brandy.

Put a dollop of topping and a cherry on each cupcake. Top with grated chocolate, dust with cocoa, and serve.

. . .

If you liked this recipe. you will love these as well.

RED VELVET CUPCAKES

CHOCOLATE RASPBERRY CUPCAKES

BLACK FOREST CHEESECAKE

. . . . .

These rich chocolate cupcakes should mimic the flavor and texture of classic brownies. Do not overbake.

CHOCOLATE BROWNIE CUPCAKES

Cupcakes

2 cups (300 g) all-purpose (plain) flour

1 teaspoon baking powder

$^1/_2$ teaspoon salt

8 ounces (250 g) dark chocolate, coarsely chopped

1 cup (250 g) unsalted butter, cut into pieces

2 cups (400 g) sugar

4 large eggs

2 teaspoons vanilla extract (essence)

Chocolate Buttercream

8 ounces (250 g) dark chocolate, coarsely chopped

1 cup (200 g) sugar

3 large egg whites

$^3/_4$ cups (180 g) unsalted butter, cut into small pieces

Cupcakes: Preheat the oven to 350°F (180°C/gas 4). Line a standard 12-cup muffin pan with paper liners. Butter an 8-inch (20-cm) square baking pan and line the base with parchment paper. Butter the paper.

Sift the flour, baking powder, and salt into a bowl. Combine the chocolate and butter in a double boiler over barely simmering water, stirring until melted and smooth. Set aside to cool a little.

Add the sugar to the bowl with the chocolate and beat with an electric mixer on medium-high speed until smooth. Add the eggs one at a time, beating until just combined after each addition. Beat in the vanilla.

With the mixer on low speed, beat in the flour mixture. Spoon the batter into the paper liners, filling each one two-thirds full. Spoon the remaining batter into the prepared pan, spreading it in an even layer.

Bake the cupcakes for 18–20 minutes, until just set but still soft. Let the cupcakes cool in the pan for 5 minutes. Turn out onto wire racks and let cool completely, about 1 hour.

Bake the extra batter for about 15 minutes, until just set on top. Place the pan on a wire rack to cool.

Chocolate Buttercream: Melt the chocolate in a double boiler over barely simmering water, or in the microwave. Let cool a little.

Combine the sugar and egg whites in a double boiler over barely simmering water. Whisk constantly until the mixture is heated and the sugar is dissolved.

Remove from the heat and beat with an electric mixer until cooled and stiff peaks form. With the mixer running, add the butter, one piece at a time, beating until fully incorporated. Continue beating until a light, fluffy cream has formed. Stir in the chocolate until well combined.

Put the buttercream in a pastry (piping) bag and frost the cupcakes. Crumble the extra brownie batter in the cake pan, sprinkle some over each cupcake, and serve.

Makes: 12 cupcakes
Preparation: 30 minutes
   + 1 hour to cool
Cooking: 20–25 minutes
Level: 1

CHOCOLATE STRAWBERRY CUPCAKES

Cupcakes

- 1¹⁄₂ cups (225 g) all-purpose (plain) flour,
- 1¹⁄₂ teaspoons baking powder
- ³⁄₄ teaspoon salt
- ¹⁄₂ cup (120 g) unsalted butter, softened
- ³⁄₄ cup (150 g) sugar
- 2 large eggs
- 1 teaspoon vanilla extract (essence)
- ¹⁄₂ cup (120 ml) milk

Frosting

- 1 cup (150 g) confectioners' (icing) sugar
- ¹⁄₄ cup (30 g) unsweetened cocoa powder
- ¹⁄₄ teaspoon salt
- ¹⁄₂ cup (120 g) unsalted butter, softened
- 2 tablespoons milk
- ¹⁄₂ teaspoon vanilla extract (essence)
- ¹⁄₃ cup (120 g) seedless strawberry preserves (jam)
- 12 small strawberries, sliced, to decorate

Cupcakes: Preheat the oven to 350°F (180°C/gas 4). Line a standard 12-cup muffin pan with paper liners.

Sift the flour, baking powder, and salt into a bowl. Beat the butter and sugar in a bowl with an electric mixer on medium-high speed until pale and creamy. Add the eggs one at a time, beating until just combined after each addition. Beat in the vanilla.

With the mixer on low speed, gradually beat in the flour mixture, alternating with the milk. Spoon the batter into the paper liners, filling each one two-thirds full.

Bake for 20–25 minutes, until a toothpick inserted into the centers comes out clean. Let the cupcakes cool in the pan for 5 minutes. Turn out onto wire racks and let cool completely, about 1 hour.

Frosting: Sift the confectioners' sugar, cocoa, and salt into a bowl. Beat the butter with a mixer on medium speed until pale and fluffy. With the mixer on low speed, gradually beat in the cocoa mixture, milk, and vanilla.

Using a small sharp knife, cut a 1-inch (2.5-cm) deep hole from the top of each cupcake (do not discard). Fill each hole with strawberry preserves and replace the cutout pieces.

Spread the cupcakes with the frosting. Decorate with the strawberries, and serve.

. . .

If you liked this recipe, you will love these as well.

WHITE CHOCOLATE CUPCAKES WITH STRAWBERRIES

CHOCOLATE RASPBERRY CUPCAKES

CHOCOLATE VULCANO CUPCAKES

Makes: 12 cupcakes
Preparation: 40 minutes
  + 1 hour to cool
Cooking: 20–25 minutes
Level: 2

WHITE CHOCOLATE CUPCAKES
with strawberries

Cupcakes

1 1/3	cups (200 g) all-purpose (plain) flour
1	teaspoon baking powder
1/4	teaspoon baking soda (bicarbonate of soda)
1/2	teaspoon salt
1/2	cup (100 g) sugar
1/4	cup (50 g) packed dark brown sugar
4	ounces (120 g) white chocolate, chopped
1/2	cup (90 ml) vegetable oil
3/4	cup (180 ml) cup coconut milk
2	teaspoons vanilla extract (essence)
1/2	teaspoon finely grated unwaxed lemon zest

Frosting

1/2	cup (120 g) butter, softened
1/3	cup (90 g) cream cheese, softened
3	cups (450 g) confectioners' (icing) sugar
6	ounces (180 g) white chocolate, melted
1	teaspoon vanilla extract (essence)
1	tablespoon milk
	Few drops red food coloring
6	strawberries, sliced

Cupcakes: Preheat the oven to 350°F (180°C/gas 4). Line a standard 12-cup muffin pan with paper liners.

Sift the flour, baking powder, baking soda, and salt into a bowl. Stir in both sugars.

Melt the white chocolate in a double boiler over barely simmering water, or in the microwave. Mix the melted chocolate and oil in a bowl. Whisk the coconut milk, vanilla, and lemon zest in a bowl.

Make a well in the center of the flour mixture and pour in the chocolate mixture and the coconut mixture. Stir with a wooden spoon until smooth. Spoon the batter into the paper liners, filling each one two-thirds full.

Bake for 20–25 minutes, until golden and a toothpick inserted into the centers comes out clean. Let the cupcakes cool in the pan for 5 minutes. Turn out onto wire racks and let cool completely, about 1 hour.

Frosting: Beat the butter and cream cheese in a bowl with an electric mixer on medium speed until pale and fluffy. With the mixer on low speed, gradually add the confectioners' sugar, beating until creamy.

Melt the white chocolate in a double boiler over barely simmering water, or in the microwave. Stir in the vanilla and let cool for a few minutes.

Add the white chocolate to the frosting, mixing well. Add the milk and beat until fluffy.

Divide the frosting evenly between two bowls. Tint one bowl of frosting bright red.

Fill a pastry (piping) bag with a star-shaped nozzle with the plain frosting and pipe over six cupcakes. Clean the pastry bag and fill with the red frosting. Pipe over the remaining cupcakes.

Top each cupcake with a slice or two of strawberry, and serve.

Makes: 12 cupcakes
Preparation: 30 minutes
+ 1 hour to cool
Cooking: 20–25 minutes
Level: 2

• • • • •

These pretty cupcakes are not hard to make.
They are perfect for a little girl's birthday party.

CHOCOLATE BUTTERFLY CUPCAKES

Cupcakes

³/₄	cup (125 g) all-purpose (plain) flour
1¹/₂	teaspoons baking powder
1	tablespoon unsweetened cocoa powder
¹/₄	teaspoon salt
¹/₂	cup (120 g) unsalted butter, softened
²/₃	cup (125 g) sugar
2	large eggs

Frosting

¹/₂	cup (120 g) unsalted butter, softened
1²/₃	cups (250 g) confectioners' (icing) sugar + extra, for dusting
1	teaspoon hot water
¹/₂	teaspoon vanilla extract (essence)
	Few drops of red, blue, and yellow food coloring
	Candy-coated chocolate (M&M's or Smarties), for eyes
	Fruit jellies and licorice lace, sliced, for feelers

Cupcakes: Preheat the oven to 350°F (180°C/gas 4). Line a standard 12-cup muffin pan with paper liners.

Sift the flour, baking powder, cocoa, and salt into a bowl. Beat the butter and sugar in a large bowl with an electric mixer on medium-high speed until pale and creamy. Add the eggs one at a time, beating until just combined after each addition.

With the mixer on low speed, gradually beat in the flour mixture. Spoon the batter into the paper liners, filling each one two-thirds full.

Bake for 20–25 minutes, until golden brown and firm to the touch. Transfer the muffin pan to a wire rack. Let the cupcakes cool in the pan for 5 minutes. Turn out onto wire racks and let cool completely, about 1 hour.

Frosting: Beat the butter in a bowl with an electric mixer until creamy. Gradually beat in the confectioners' sugar until smooth and creamy. Stir in the water and vanilla. Divide the frosting evenly among three small bowls and stir red food coloring into one, blue food coloring into another, and yellow food coloring into the third.

Cut the rounded top off each cupcake. Dust the tops with confectioners' sugar, then cut each one in half to make two "wings."

Spread four cupcakes with red frosting, four with blue, and four with yellow. Arrange a pair of wings on each cupcake. Add candy-coated chocolate for the eyes and slices of fruit jellies or licorice to make feelers. Let set for a few minutes, then serve.

• • •

If you liked this recipe, you will love these as well.

BLACK FOREST
CUPCAKES

MINI CHOCOLATE
CUPCAKES WITH
RAINBOW FROSTING

CHOCOLATE SWIRL
CUPCAKES

Makes: 12 cupcakes
Preparation: 30 minutes
   + 1 hour to cool
Cooking: 25–30 minutes
Level: 1

. . . . .

The topping on these cupcakes is inspired by the famous Florentine cookies. Wrap the finished cupcakes in fancy paper liners and serve on special occasions.

FLORENTINE CUPCAKES

Cupcakes

3   ounces (90 g) dark chocolate, coarsely chopped
1/3 cup (90 ml) light (single) cream
2/3 cup (100 g) all-purpose (plain) flour
1/2 cup (50 g) finely ground almonds
2   tablespoons unsweetened cocoa powder
1   teaspoon baking powder
1/3 cup (90 g) salted butter, softened
1   cup (200 g) firmly packed brown sugar
2   large eggs

Chocolate Ganache

4   ounces (120 g) dark chocolate, chopped
1/4 cup (60 ml) light (single) cream

Topping

3/4 cup (120 g) slivered almonds
2/3 cup (120 g) candied (glacé) cherries, coarsely chopped
1/4 cup (45 g) candied (glacé) ginger, coarsely chopped
2   tablespoons candied (glacé) orange peel
2   ounces (60 g) dark chocolate, coarsely chopped

Cupcakes: Preheat the oven to 325°F (170°C/gas 3). Line a standard 12-cup muffin pan with paper liners.

Melt the chocolate and cream in a double boiler over barely simmering water. Combine the flour, almonds, cocoa, and baking powder in a small bowl. Beat the butter and brown sugar in a medium bowl with an electric mixer on medium-high speed until creamy. Add the eggs one at a time, beating until just blended after each addition. With the mixer on low speed, gradually beat in the flour mixture and melted chocolate.

Spoon the batter into the paper liners, filling each one two-thirds full.

Bake for 25–30 minutes, until risen and firm to the touch. Let the cupcakes cool in the pan for 5 minutes. Turn out onto wire racks and let cool completely, about 1 hour.

Chocolate Ganache: Melt the chocolate and cream in a double boiler over barely simmering water, or in the microwave. Let cool.

Spread on the cupcakes.

Topping: Combine the almonds, cherries, ginger, and orange peel in a small bowl. Cover the tops of the cupcakes with this mixture.

Melt the chocolate in a double boiler over barely simmering water. Drizzle over the cupcakes and serve.

. . .

If you liked this recipe, you will love these as well.

FLORENTINE STARS

CHOCOLATE BROWNIE CUPCAKES

CHOCOLATE HAZELNUT CUPCAKES

. . . . .

You could also decorate these cupcakes with tiny chocolate or candy Easter bunnies.

CHOCOLATE EASTER CUPCAKES

Cupcakes

1½	cups (225 g) all-purpose (plain) flour
¼	cup (30 g) unsweetened cocoa powder
1	teaspoon baking powder
½	teaspoon baking soda (bicarbonate of soda)
7	ounces (200 g) milk chocolate, chopped
¾	cup (180 g) salted butter, softened
1	cup (200 g) superfine (caster) sugar
3	large eggs
½	cup (120 ml) milk
20	small chocolate Easter eggs, to decorate (optional)

Frosting

⅓	cup (90 g) salted butter, softened
⅓	cup (50 g) unsweetened cocoa powder
3	cups (450 g) confectioners' (icing) sugar
¼	cup (60 ml) milk

Cupcakes: Preheat the oven to 350°F (180°C/gas 4). Line 20 cups in two standard 12-cup muffin pans with paper liners.

Sift the flour, cocoa, baking powder, and baking soda into a bowl.

Melt the chocolate in a double boiler over barely simmering water, or in the microwave. Set aside for 5 minutes to cool slightly.

Beat the butter and sugar in a large bowl with an electric mixer on medium-high speed until pale and creamy. Add the eggs one at a time, beating until just combined after each addition.

With the mixer on low speed, add the chocolate and beat until well combined. Gradually beat in the flour mixture, alternating with the milk.

Spoon the batter into the paper liners, filling each one two-thirds full.

Bake for 20–25 minutes, until a toothpick inserted into the centers comes out clean. Let the cupcakes cool in the pan for 5 minutes. Turn out onto wire racks and let cool completely, about 1 hour.

Frosting: Beat the butter in a bowl with the mixer on medium speed until very pale. Gradually add the cocoa, confectioners' sugar, and milk, beating until well combined.

Spread the frosting over the top of each cupcake. Top with an Easter egg, if liked, and let stand until set.

. . .

If you liked this recipe, you will love these as well.

134
CHOCOLATE BUTTERFLY
CUPCAKES

140
VANILLA CUPCAKE PARTY

144
CHOCOLATE CUPCAKE
CONES

Makes: 12 cupcakes

Preparation: 20 minutes
+ 1½ hours to cool
& chill

Cooking: 20–25 minutes

Level: 1

VANILLA CUPCAKE PARTY

Cupcakes

³⁄₄	cup (200 g) unsalted butter
1	cup (200 g) firmly packed light brown sugar
3	large eggs
1½	teaspoons vanilla extract (essence)
1¼	cups (180 g) all-purpose flour
1	tablespoon unsweetened cocoa powder
1	teaspoon baking powder
½	teaspoon baking soda (bicarbonate of soda)
2	ounces (60 g) white or dark chocolate, coarsely chopped
3	tablespoons milk

Frosting

3½	ounces (100 g) white chocolate
7	ounces (200 g) cream cheese, softened
¼	cup (60 g) unsalted butter, softened
1	teaspoon vanilla extract (essence)
1²⁄₃	cups (250 g) confectioners' sugar
	Chocolate sprinkles, to decorate

Cupcakes: Preheat the oven to 350°F (180°C/gas 4). Line a standard 12-cup muffin pan with paper liners.

Put all the ingredients except for the chocolate and milk into a food processor and chop until smooth. Stir in the chocolate and milk.

Spoon the batter into the paper liners, filling each one two-thirds full.

Bake for 20–25 minutes, until risen and springy to the touch. Let the cupcakes cool in the pan for 5 minutes. Turn out onto wire racks and let cool completely, about 1 hour.

Frosting: Melt the white chocolate in a double boiler over barely simmering water, or in the microwave. Let cool slightly.

Beat the cream cheese in a bowl with an electric mixer on medium speed until soft and smooth. Beat in the butter and vanilla, followed by the confectioners' sugar and then the white chocolate. Chill for 30 minutes.

Spread the frosting on the cupcakes. Finish with the chocolate sprinkles, and serve.

. . .

If you liked this recipe, you will love these as well.

RED VELVET CUPCAKES

BLACK FOREST CUPCAKES

CHOCOLATE BROWNIE CUPCAKES

Makes: 60–65 mini cupcakes

Preparation: 45 minutes + 1 hour to cool

Cooking: 10 minutes

Level: 1

. . . . .

These pretty little cupcakes are perfect for a children's birthday party or a buffet spread for a large party. Make as many different colored frostings as you like. The more the merrier!

MINI CHOCOLATE CUPCAKES
with rainbow frosting

Cupcakes
3/4	cup (120 g) unsweetened cocoa powder
1 1/2	cups (225 g) all-purpose (plain) flour
1 1/2	cups (300 g) sugar
1 1/2	teaspoons baking soda (bicarbonate of soda)
3/4	teaspoon baking powder
3/4	teaspoon salt
2	large eggs, lightly beaten
3/4	cup (180 ml) warm water
3/4	cup (180 ml) buttermilk
3	tablespoons safflower oil
1	teaspoon vanilla extract (essence)

Buttercream
12	ounces (350 g) unsalted butter, softened
1	pound (500 g) confectioners' (icing) sugar, sifted
1/2	teaspoon vanilla extract (essence)
	Few drops each red, green, and yellow food coloring

Cupcakes: Preheat the oven to 350°F (180°C/gas 4). Line 60–65 mini-muffin pans with paper liners.

Combine the cocoa, flour, sugar, baking soda, baking powder, and salt in a large bowl. Add the eggs, warm water, buttermilk, oil, and vanilla, and mix with a wooden spoon or electric mixer until smooth.

Spoon the batter into the paper liners, filling each one two-thirds full.

Bake for 10 minutes, until the tops spring back when touched. Let cool in the pan for 5 minutes. Turn out onto wire racks and let cool completely, about 1 hour.

Buttercream: Beat the butter with an electric mixer on medium-high speed until pale and creamy. With the mixer on low speed, gradually beat in the confectioners' sugar. Add the vanilla and beat until smooth and creamy.

Divide the frosting among three bowls. Add the different colored food coloring drop by drop to each bowl to make bright colors.

Place one colored frosting in a pastry (piping) bag and pipe over some of the cupcakes. Clean the pastry bag and repeat with the other colors until all the cupcakes are frosted. Let set for a few minutes before serving.

. . .

If you liked this recipe, you will love these as well.

CHOCOLATE STRAWBERRY CUPCAKES

CHOCOLATE BUTTERFLY CUPCAKES

CHOCOLATE MINT CUPCAKES

Makes: 12 cupcakes

Preparation: 30 minutes
+ 1 hour to cool

Cooking: 20–25 minutes

Level: 2

CHOCOLATE CUPCAKE CONES

Cupcakes

- 1¼ cups (180 g) all-purpose (plain) flour
- 1 teaspoon baking powder
- 1 teaspoon ground cinnamon
- ¼ teaspoon salt
- ½ cup (120 g) unsalted butter, softened
- ¾ cup (150 g) sugar
- ½ teaspoon vanilla extract (essence)
- 2 large eggs
- ⅓ cup (90 ml) milk
- 1 cup (150 g) fresh or frozen (thawed) raspberries
- 12 flat-bottom ice cream cone cups

Frosting

- ½ cup (125 g) unsalted butter, softened
- ½ teaspoon vanilla extract (essence)
- 1½ cups (225 g) confectioners' (icing) sugar
- 3 tablespoons unsweetened cocoa powder
- Chocolate Flake bars, or other crumbly chocolate bars, to decorate

Cupcakes: Preheat the oven to 350°F (180°C/gas 4). Line a standard 12-cup muffin pan with paper liners.

Sift the flour, baking powder, cinnamon, and salt into a bowl. Beat the butter, sugar, and vanilla in a medium bowl with an electric mixer on medium-high speed until pale and creamy. Add the eggs one at a time, beating until just blended after each addition.

With the mixer on low speed, add the flour mixture, alternating with the milk. Stir the raspberries in by hand.

Spoon the batter into the prepared cups, filling each one two-thirds full.

Bake for 20–25 minutes, until golden brown and firm to the touch. Transfer the muffin pan to a wire rack. Let the cupcakes cool in the pan for 5 minutes. Turn out onto wire racks and let cool completely, about 1 hour.

Remove the paper cases from the cupcakes. Shape the bottoms of the cakes with a serrated knife so that they sit inside the ice cream cones. Place the cupcakes in the cones.

Frosting: Beat the butter and vanilla in a small bowl with an electric mixer until creamy. Gradually add the confectioners' sugar and cocoa, beating until combined.

Spread the frosting over the cupcakes. Decorate with the crumbled chocolate bars, and serve.

. . .

If you liked this recipe, you will love these as well.

MINI CHOCOLATE CUPCAKES WITH RAINBOW FROSTING

142

CHOCOLATE PEANUT CUPCAKES

149

CHOCOLATE SWIRL CUPCAKES

152

Makes: 18 cupcakes
Preparation: 30 minutes
+ 1 hour to cool
Cooking: 20–25 minutes
Level: 2

CHOCOLATE MINT CUPCAKES

Cupcakes

2	cups (300 g) all-purpose (plain) flour
1/2	cup (75 g) unsweetened cocoa powder
1	teaspoon baking powder
1/2	teaspoon baking soda (bicarbonate of soda)
1/4	teaspoon salt
2/3	cup (150 g) unsalted butter, softened
1 1/2	cups (300 g) sugar
3	large eggs
3/4	cup (180 ml) milk
1	teaspoon peppermint extract (essence)
12	chocolate cream after-dinner mints, chopped

Chocolate Glaze

6	ounces (180 g) dark chocolate, chopped
1/2	cup (120 g) unsalted butter, cut up
1	teaspoon peppermint extract (essence)
	Shards of chocolate, to decorate

Cupcakes: Preheat the oven to 350°F (180°C/gas 4). Line a standard 12-cup muffin pan and a standard 6-cup muffin pan with paper liners.

Sift the flour, cocoa, baking powder, baking soda, and salt into a large bowl.

Beat the butter and sugar in a bowl with an electric mixer on medium-high speed until creamy. Add the eggs one at a time, beating until just blended after each addition.

With the mixer on low speed, beat in the flour mixture, alternating with the milk and peppermint extract. Stir in the chopped chocolate mints by hand.

Spoon the batter into the paper liners, filling each one two-thirds full.

Bake for 20–25 minutes, until risen and firm to the touch. Let the cupcakes cool in the pan for 5 minutes. Turn out onto wire racks and let cool completely, about 1 hour.

Chocolate Glaze: Melt the chocolate and butter in a double boiler over barely simmering water. Stir in the peppermint extract. Set aside to cool a little.

Drizzle the glaze over the cupcakes, decorate with the shards of chocolate, and serve.

. . .

If you liked this recipe,
you will love these as well.

CHOCOLATE MINT CREAMS

CHOCOLATE MINT BARS

CHOCOLATE MINT HEARTS

Makes: 12 cupcakes
Preparation: 30 minutes
    + 1 hour to cool
Cooking: 30–35 minutes
Level: 2

CHOCOLATE PEANUT CUPCAKES

Cupcakes

3	ounces (90 g) dark chocolate, coarsely chopped
1/4	cup (60 ml) light (single) cream
2/3	cup (160 g) smooth peanut butter, softened
2/3	cup (100 g) all-purpose (plain) flour
3	tablespoons unsweetened cocoa powder
1	teaspoon baking powder
1/4	teaspoon salt
1/2	cup (50 g) finely ground almonds
1/4	cup (60 g) unsalted butter, softened
1	cup (200 g) firmly packed light brown sugar
2	large eggs

Peanut Praline

1/3	cup (70 g) sugar
1/2	cup (50 g) blanched peanuts, coarsely chopped
3	ounces (90 g) dark chocolate, coarsely chopped

Cupcakes: Preheat the oven to 350°F (180°C/gas 4). Line a standard 12-cup muffin pan with paper liners.

Melt the chocolate, cream, and peanut butter in a double boiler over barely simmering water, stirring until smooth. Remove from the heat and let cool.

Sift the flour, cocoa, baking powder, and salt into a small bowl. Stir in the almonds.

Beat the butter and brown sugar in a medium bowl with an electric mixer on medium-high speed until creamy. Add the eggs one at a time, beating until just blended after each addition. With the mixer on low speed, gradually beat in the flour mixture and melted chocolate mixture.

Spoon the batter into the paper liners, filling each one two-thirds full.

Bake for 20–25 minutes, until risen and firm to the touch. Let the cupcakes cool in the pan for 5 minutes. Turn out onto wire racks and let cool completely, about 1 hour.

Peanut Praline: Line a baking sheet with parchment paper. Put the sugar in a small pan and heat gently until melted and pale gold, about 5 minutes. Add the peanuts and cook, stirring, for 30 seconds. Pour onto the prepared baking sheet and leave to harden. Break into small shards.

Melt the chocolate in a double boiler over barely simmering water, or in the microwave. Remove from the heat and let cool a little. Spread some chocolate on each cupcake. Decorate with the peanut praline, and serve.

. . .

*If you liked this recipe,
you will love these as well.*

BROWN SUGAR
BROWNIES WITH
CHOCOLATE & NUTS

FLORENTINE CUPCAKES

CHOCOLATE HAZELNUT
CUPCAKES

Makes: 12 cupcakes
Preparation: 30 minutes
+ 1 hour to cool
Cooking: 25–30 minutes
Level: 2

. . . . .

Replace the hazelnuts in this recipe with the same quantity of almonds or walnuts for an equally delicious cupcake.

CHOCOLATE HAZELNUT CUPCAKES

Cupcakes

$3^1/_2$ ounces (100 g) dark chocolate, coarsely chopped

$1/_3$ cup (90 ml) light (single) cream

$2/_3$ cup (100 g) all-purpose (plain) flour

2 tablespoons unsweetened cocoa powder

1 teaspoon baking powder

$1/_8$ teaspoon salt

$1/_2$ cup (50 g) finely ground hazelnuts

$1/_3$ cup (90 g) unsalted butter, softened

1 cup (200 g) firmly packed light brown sugar

2 large eggs

1 tablespoon hazelnut liqueur

$1/_4$ cup (40 g) hazelnuts, coarsely chopped

Frosting

$3^1/_2$ ounces (100 g) dark chocolate, coarsely chopped

$1/_2$ cup (120 g) chocolate hazelnut spread (Nutella)

2 tablespoons coarsely chopped hazelnuts, to decorate

Cupcakes: Preheat the oven to 325°F (170°C/gas 3). Line a standard 12-cup muffin pan with paper liners.

Melt the chocolate and cream in a double boiler over barely simmering water, stirring until smooth. Remove from the heat and let cool.

Sift the flour, cocoa, baking powder, and salt into a small bowl. Stir in the ground hazelnuts.

Beat the butter and brown sugar in a medium bowl with an electric mixer on medium-high speed until creamy. Add the eggs in one at a time, beating until just blended after each addition.

With the mixer on low speed, gradually beat in the flour mixture and chocolate mixture. Stir in the hazelnut liqueur and chopped hazelnuts by hand.

Spoon the batter into the paper liners, filling each one two-thirds full.

Bake for 25–30 minutes, until risen and firm to the touch. Let the cupcakes cool in the pan for 5 minutes. Turn out onto wire racks and let cool completely, about 1 hour.

Frosting: Melt the chocolate in a double boiler over barely simmering water, or in the microwave. Remove from the heat and stir in the chocolate hazelnut spread. Let cool a little.

Spoon the mixture into a pastry (piping) bag fitted with a star-shaped nozzle and pipe a swirl of frosting on each cupcake. Sprinkle with the coarsely chopped hazelnuts, and serve.

. . .

If you liked this recipe, you will love these as well.

CHOCOLATE PEANUT CUPCAKES

CHOCOLATE SWIRL CUPCAKES

CHOCOLATE VULCANO CUPCAKES

Makes: 12 cupcakes
Preparation: 30 minutes
    + 1 hour to cool
Cooking: 25–30 minutes
Level: 2

CHOCOLATE SWIRL CUPCAKES

Cupcakes

1	ounce (30 g) dark chocolate, coarsely chopped
2	tablespoons light (single) cream
1	cup (150 g) all-purpose (plain) flour
1	teaspoon baking powder
$^1/_8$	teaspoon salt
$^1/_3$	cup (90 g) unsalted butter, softened
1	cup (200 g) sugar
1	teaspoon vanilla extract (essence)
2	large eggs
2	tablespoons milk
1	tablespoon unsweetened cocoa powder, sifted

Butter Frosting

$^1/_2$	cup (120 g) unsalted butter, softened
$^1/_2$	teaspoon vanilla extract (essence)
$1^1/_2$	cups (225 g) confectioners' (icing) sugar
1	tablespoon unsweetened cocoa powder

Cupcakes: Preheat the oven to 325°F (170°C/gas 3). Line a standard 12-cup muffin pan with paper liners.

Melt the chocolate and cream in a double boiler over barely simmering water, stirring until smooth. Remove from the heat and let cool.

Sift the flour, baking powder, and salt into a small bowl.

Beat the butter, sugar, and vanilla in a medium bowl with an electric mixer on medium-high speed until pale and creamy. Add the eggs one at a time, beating until just blended after each addition.

With the mixer on low speed, gradually beat in the flour mixture. Divide the batter between two bowls. Stir the milk into one bowl and the chocolate mixture and cocoa into the other. Spoon the batters alternately into the prepared cups, filling each one two-thirds full. Create a swirl pattern through the batter using a toothpick.

Bake for 25–30 minutes, until golden brown and firm to the touch. Let the cupcakes cool in the pan for 5 minutes. Turn out onto wire racks and let cool completely, about 1 hour.

Butter Frosting: Beat the butter and vanilla in a small bowl with an electric mixer on medium speed until light and fluffy. Gradually add the confectioners' sugar, beating until well combined.

Divide the frosting between two bowls. Add the cocoa to one to make chocolate frosting. Place alternate spoonfuls of vanilla and chocolate frosting into a pastry bag fitted with a star nozzle. Pipe a swirl on top of each cupcake, and serve.

. . .

If you liked this recipe, you will love these as well.

MINI CHOCOLATE
CUPCAKES WITH
RAINBOW FROSTING

CHOCOLATE PEANUT
CUPCAKES

CHOCOLATE HAZELNUT
CUPCAKES

· · · · ·

These pretty cupcakes make a wonderful dessert. Prepare an hour or two ahead of time and chill until ready to serve. Replace the raspberries with blueberries or blackberries for a change.

CHOCOLATE RASPBERRY CUPCAKES

Cupcakes

$3^1/_2$ ounces (100 g) dark chocolate, coarsely chopped

$^1/_3$ cup (90 ml) light (single) cream

$^2/_3$ cup (100 g) all-purpose (plain) flour

2 tablespoons unsweetened cocoa

1 teaspoon baking powder

$^1/_8$ teaspoon salt

$^1/_2$ cup (50 g) finely ground almonds

$^1/_3$ cup (90 g) unsalted butter

1 cup (200 g) sugar

2 large eggs

1 cup (150 g) fresh raspberries

Sugared Raspberries

1 cup (150 g) fresh raspberries

1 large egg white, lightly beaten

2 tablespoons sugar

Chocolate Buttercream

$3^1/_2$ ounces (100 g) dark chocolate

$^1/_2$ cup (120 g) unsalted butter

$^1/_2$ teaspoon vanilla extract (essence)

$^1/_2$ tablespoon milk

1 cup (150 g) confectioners' (icing) sugar

Cupcakes: Preheat the oven to 325°F (170°C/gas 3). Line a standard 12-cup muffin pan with paper liners.

Melt the chocolate and cream in a double boiler over barely simmering water, stirring until smooth. Remove from the heat and let cool.

Sift the flour, cocoa, baking powder, and salt into a small bowl. Stir in the almonds.

Beat the butter and sugar in a medium bowl with an electric mixer on medium-high speed until pale and creamy. Add the eggs one at a time, beating until just blended after each addition.

With the mixer on low speed, gradually beat in the flour mixture and chocolate mixture. Stir the raspberries in by hand.

Spoon the batter into the paper liners, filling each one two-thirds full.

Bake for 25–30 minutes, until golden brown and firm to the touch. Let cool in the pan for 5 minutes. Turn out onto wire racks and let cool completely, about 1 hour.

Sugared Raspberries: Line a baking sheet with parchment paper. Brush each raspberry with egg white and roll in the sugar. Place the raspberries on the prepared baking sheet and leave to dry.

Chocolate Buttercream: Melt the chocolate in a double boiler over barely simmering water, or in the microwave. Let cool.

Beat the butter and vanilla in a medium bowl with an electric mixer on medium speed until pale and creamy. Beat in the milk and cooled chocolate. Gradually add the confectioners' sugar, beating until blended.

Put the buttercream in a pastry (piping) bag and pipe swirls on the cupcakes. Top with the sugared raspberries, and serve.

Makes: 12 cupcakes
Preparation: 30 minutes
    + 1 hour to cool
Cooking: 20–25 minutes
Level: 2

CHOCOLATE VULCANO CUPCAKES

Cupcakes

1 cup (150 g) all-purpose (plain) flour

3 tablespoons unsweetened cocoa powder

1 teaspoon baking powder

1/4 teaspoon salt

1/2 cup (120 g) unsalted butter, softened

3/4 cup (150 g) firmly packed dark brown sugar

1/2 teaspoon vanilla extract (essence)

2 large eggs

3 tablespoons milk

1/3 cup (120 g) raspberry preserves (jam)

Chocolate Buttercream

6 ounces (180 g) dark chocolate

1 cup (250 g) unsalted butter, softened

1/2 teaspoon vanilla extract (essence)

1 tablespoon milk

2 cups (300 g) confectioners' (icing) sugar

1/2 cup (150 g) raspberry preserves (jam), strained

Hot water

Cupcakes: Preheat the oven to 350°F (180°C/gas 4). Line a standard 12-cup muffin pan with paper liners.

Sift the flour, cocoa, baking powder, and salt into a small bowl.

Beat the butter, brown sugar, and vanilla in a medium bowl with an electric mixer on medium-high speed until creamy. Add the eggs one at a time, beating until just blended after each addition.

With the mixer on low speed, add the flour mixture, alternating with the milk. Spoon half the batter into the prepared cups. Place some raspberry preserves in the center of each one and spoon the remaining batter over the top.

Bake for 20–25 minutes, until risen and firm to the touch. Let the cupcakes cool in the pan for 5 minutes. Turn out onto wire racks and let cool completely, about 1 hour.

Chocolate Buttercream: Melt the chocolate in a double boiler over barely simmering water. Remove from the heat and let cool.

Beat the butter and vanilla in a bowl with an electric mixer on medium-high speed until pale and creamy. Pour in the milk and cooled chocolate, beating until blended. Gradually beat in the confectioners' sugar until smooth.

Pile the frosting on top of each cupcake to create a volcano shape. Make a crater-like indent at the top. Thin down the raspberry preserves with a little hot water. Spoon the raspberry preserves into the top of each "volcano," allowing it to run down the sides a little, like magma.

. . .

If you liked this recipe, you will love these as well.

150

CHOCOLATE HAZELNUT
CUPCAKES

152

CHOCOLATE SWIRL
CUPCAKES

155

CHOCOLATE RASPBERRY
CUPCAKES

cakes & rolls

Here you will find 22 ideas for cakes, from simple recipes like Chocolate apple cake and Quick marble cake, to sophisticated offerings, such as Dobos torte and Sachertorte.

Serves: 8–12
Preparation: 45 minutes
Cooking: 50–60 minutes
Level: 2

· · · · ·

Granny Smiths are always a good choice for baking. They are almost always easy to find, even when out of season locally.

CHOCOLATE APPLE CAKE

Filling

1½	pounds (750 g) apples
	Finely grated zest and juice of 1 large unwaxed orange
2	tablespoons sugar
1	teaspoon unsalted butter
¼	cup (50 g) golden raisins (sultanas)
3½	ounces (100 g) dark chocolate, grated

Crumble

1	cup (150 g) all-purpose (plain) flour
½	cup (100 g) sugar
⅔	cup (60 g) finely ground almonds
½	cup (120 g) salted butter, softened
1–2	tablespoons cream

Cake

1	cup (250 g) salted butter, softened
1	cup (150 g) light brown sugar
3	large eggs
1⅔	cups (250 g) all-purpose (plain) flour
1	teaspoon baking powder
4	tablespoons coffee mixed with 1 teaspoon cocoa
¾	cup (120 g) almonds, chopped
2	ounces (60 g) dark chocolate, grated

Filling: Peel and core the apples and slice thickly. Place in a heavy-based saucepan with the orange zest and juice. Add the sugar, butter, and golden raisins, partially cover the pan, and simmer for 8–10 minutes, stirring occasionally until the apples are slightly softened. Add 1–2 tablespoons of water, if needed.

Set aside to cool completely, then stir in the chocolate.

Crumble: Mix the flour, sugar, and almonds in a bowl. Rub in the butter with your fingers, until combined. Spoon in the cream and rub through the mixture until it is crumbly.

Preheat the oven to 325°F (170°C/gas 3). Generously butter the bottom and sides of a 9-inch (23-cm) square baking pan.

Cake: Beat the butter and brown sugar in a bowl with an electric mixer on medium-high speed until creamy. Add the eggs one at a time, beating until just combined after each addition.

Sift the flour and baking powder into a bowl. Fold into the batter, along with the coffee mixture. Fold in the almonds and chocolate. Spoon the batter into the pan.

Spread the apple filling over the cake mixture. Break up the crumble with a fork and sprinkle evenly over the apple filling.

Bake for 50–60 minutes, until golden brown on top. Let cool completely in the pan. Cut into squares, and serve.

· · ·

If you liked this recipe, you will love these as well.

162
CHOCOLATE CAKE
WITH BEETS

166
PEAR & HAZELNUT
CHOCOLATE CAKE

195
CHOCOLATE BANANA
ROULADE WITH HONEY-
COMB CHOCOLATE

Serves: 8-10
Preparation: 30 minutes
    + 1-12 hours to chill
Cooking: 1 hour
Level: 1

. . . . .

You will be pleasantly surprised by this cake; the beets are a wonderful addition, adding depth of flavor and texture. For the best results, prepare the cake a day ahead and glaze just before serving. The cake becomes more moist and flavorsome if stored overnight in an airtight container.

CHOCOLATE CAKE
with beets

Cake

1½	cups (225 g) all-purpose (plain) flour
¼	cup (30 g) unsweetened cocoa powder
1	teaspoon baking powder
1	teaspoon baking soda (bicarbonate of soda)
1	teaspoon pumpkin pie spice or allspice
3	large eggs, lightly beaten
1	cup (200 g) firmly packed brown sugar
½	cup (120 ml) sour cream
⅓	cup (90 ml) vegetable oil
1	teaspoon vanilla extract (essence)
2	cups (300 g) coarsely grated beets (beetroot/red beet)

Chocolate Glaze

5	ounces (150 g) dark chocolate, coarsely chopped
⅓	cup (90 ml) light (single) cream
½	teaspoon vanilla extract (essence)

Cake: Preheat the oven to 325°F (170°C/gas 3). Lightly grease a 9-inch (23-cm) springform pan. Line the base with parchment paper.

Sift the flour, cocoa, baking powder, baking soda, and pumpkin pie spice into a bowl.

Beat the eggs, brown sugar, sour cream, oil, and vanilla in a large bowl with an electric mixer on medium speed until smooth. With the mixer on low speed, beat in the flour mixture. Stir the beets in by hand.

Spoon the batter into the prepared pan, smoothing the top.

Bake for 1 hour, until a toothpick inserted into the center comes out clean. Let cool in the pan for 20 minutes, then turn out onto a wire rack and let cool completely.

Chocolate Glaze: Melt the chocolate, cream, and vanilla in a double boiler over barely simmering water, stirring occasionally until smooth. Remove from the heat and set aside to cool slightly.

Spread the glaze over the cake, allowing it to dribble down the sides. Slice and serve.

. . .

If you liked this recipe, you will love these as well.

CHOCOLATE APPLE CAKE

CHOCOLATE ROLL WITH BOOZY STRAWBERRIES

CHOCOLATE CHESTNUT MOUSSE CAKE

Serves: 10–12
Preparation: 25 minutes
Cooking: 1 hour
Level: 1

· · · · ·

This is a traditional German cake. Enjoy it with a cup of tea or coffee.

OTTILIENKUCHEN

Cake

2	tablespoons fine dry bread crumbs
1⅓	cups (200 g) all-purpose (plain) flour
⅓	cup (50 g) cornstarch (cornflour)
1	teaspoon baking powder
¼	teaspoon salt
1	cup (100 g) finely ground almonds
1	cup (250 g) unsalted butter, softened
1	cup (200 g) superfine (caster) sugar
2	teaspoons vanilla extract (essence)
4	large eggs
1½	tablespoons rum
3½	ounces (100 g) dark chocolate, coarsely chopped

Ganache

| 5 | ounces (150 g) dark chocolate, coarsely chopped |
| ⅓ | cup (90 ml) heavy (double) cream |

Cake: Preheat the oven to 375°F (190°C/gas 5). Brush a 9-inch (23-cm) bundt pan with melted butter. Sprinkle with the bread crumbs, turning to coat evenly. Shake out the excess.

Sift the flour, cornstarch, baking powder, and salt into a bowl. Stir in the almonds.

Beat the butter, sugar, and vanilla in a large bowl with an electric mixer on medium-high speed until pale and creamy. Add the eggs one at a time, beating until just combined after each addition.

With the mixer on low speed, gradually beat in the flour mixture. Add the rum and beat to combine. Stir in the chocolate by hand. Spoon the batter into the prepared pan, smoothing the surface.

Bake for 1 hour, until a toothpick inserted into the center comes out clean. Let cool in the pan for 10 minutes, then turn out onto a wire rack to cool completely.

Ganache: Place the chocolate and cream in a double boiler over barely simmering water and stir until melted and smooth. Set aside to cool slightly.

Pour the ganache over the cake, letting it drip down the sides. Let set for a few minutes. Slice and serve.

· · ·

If you liked this recipe, you will love these as well.

PRINCE REGENT TORTE

SACHERTORTE

CHOCOLATE CHERRY TORTE

QUICK MARBLE CAKE

1   cup (250 g) salted butter, softened

1¼   cups (250 g) sugar

4   large eggs

1½   cups (225 g) all-purpose (plain) flour

1½   teaspoons baking powder

3   tablespoons milk

1   teaspoon vanilla extract (essence)

2   tablespoons unsweetened cocoa powder

    Confectioners' (icing) sugar, to dust

Preheat the oven to 350°F (180°C/gas 4). Grease an 8-inch (20-cm) springform pan. Line the base with parchment paper.

Put all the ingredients except the cocoa and confectioners' sugar into a food processor and process until smooth, 1–2 minutes.

Divide the mixture evenly between two bowls. Stir the cocoa into one of the bowls.

Put alternate spoonfuls of the chocolate and plain batters into the prepared pan, smoothing the top with the spoon.

Bake for 45–55 minutes, until a toothpick inserted into the center comes out clean. Let cool in the pan for 10 minutes, then turn out onto a wire rack to cool completely.

Dust with confectioners' sugar, slice, and serve.

Serves: 8   Preparation: 10 minutes   Cooking: 45–55 minutes   Level: 1

PEAR & HAZELNUT CHOCOLATE CAKE

¾   cup (100 g) blanched hazelnuts

1   cup (150 g) all-purpose (plain) flour

1   teaspoon baking powder

¾   cup (180 g) salted butter, cut into small pieces

¾   cup (150 g) sugar

2   large eggs, beaten

5   small, ripe pears

2   ounces (60 g) dark chocolate, grated

2   tablespoons apricot preserves (jam)

Preheat the oven to 325°F (170°C/gas 3). Grease an 8-inch (20-cm) springform pan. Line the base with parchment paper.

Grind the hazelnuts in a food processor until fairly fine. Add the flour and baking powder and process briefly. Add the butter and process until it forms crumbs. Add the sugar and eggs and process briefly.

Peel, core, and chop two of the pears. Stir the pears and chocolate into the batter.

Spoon the batter into the prepared pan. Peel, core, and thinly slice the remaining pears and arrange in a concentric pattern on the top of the cake.

Bake for 50–60 minutes, until firm to the touch. Cool in the pan for 10 minutes, then turn out and onto a wire rack. Warm the apricot preserves and brush over the top. Serve warm or at room temperature.

Serves: 8–10   Preparation: 15 minutes   Cooking: 50–60 minutes   Level: 1

You can whip this cake up in just a few minutes. To vary, try adding a few drops of red or green food coloring to the plain batter. Alternatively, add a teaspoon of ground cinnamon or other spices to the plain batter.

This delicious cake is simple to prepare and very attractive. If there is any leftover, you can store it in an airtight container in the refrigerator for 1–2 days.

Serves: 8–12
Preparation: 30 minutes
Cooking: 40–45 minutes
Level: 2

FROSTED MOCHA CAKE

Cake

1³/₄	cups (275 g) all-purpose (plain) flour
²/₃	cup (100 g) unsweetened cocoa powder
1	teaspoon baking powder
1	teaspoon baking soda (bicarbonate of soda)
1³/₄	cups (350 g) firmly packed brown sugar
²/₃	cup (150 g) salted butter, softened
1	teaspoon vanilla extract (essence)
3	large eggs
1	cup (250 ml) milk
2	tablespoons very strong brewed coffee
1	tablespoon dark rum

Mocha Frosting

4	ounces (120 g) dark chocolate, chopped
³/₄	cup (180 g) salted butter, softened
3	teaspoons instant coffee granules, dissolved in 1 tablespoon boiling water
1	teaspoon vanilla extract (essence)
2	cups (300 g) confectioners' (icing) sugar
	Chocolate-coated coffee beans, to decorate

Cake: Preheat the oven to 350°F (180°C/gas 4). Lightly grease a 9-inch (23-cm) springform pan. Line the base with parchment paper.

Sift the flour, cocoa, baking powder, and baking soda into a bowl. Beat the brown sugar, butter, and vanilla in a bowl with an electric mixer on medium-high speed until creamy. Add the eggs one at a time, beating until just combined after each addition.

Combine the milk, coffee, and rum in a small bowl. With the mixer on low speed, gradually beat in the flour mixture, alternating with the milk mixture. Spoon the batter into the prepared pan.

Bake for 40–45 minutes, until golden brown and a toothpick inserted into the center comes out clean. Leave to cool in the pan for 10 minutes. Turn out onto a wire rack and let cool completely.

Mocha Frosting: Melt the chocolate in a double boiler over barely simmering water, or in the microwave. Set aside to cool.

Beat the butter in a bowl with an electric mixer on medium speed until pale. With the mixer on low speed, add the coffee mixture, vanilla, and melted chocolate, beating to combine. Beat in the confectioners' sugar until smooth and creamy.

Use a long serrated knife to cut the cake in half horizontally. Place the bottom half on a serving plate. Spread with one-third of the frosting. Place the remaining layer of cake on top and spread the top and sides with the remaining frosting. Make a decorative border with the chocolate-coated coffee beans. Slice and serve.

. . .

If you liked this recipe, you will love these as well.

CHOCOLATE COCONUT CAKE

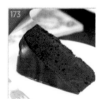

CHOCOLATE MUD CAKE

DEVIL'S FOOD CAKE

Serves: 8–10
Preparation: 30 minutes
    + 1 hour to cool
Cooking: 50–55 minutes
Level: 1

CHOCOLATE COCONUT CAKE

Cake

1½	cups (225 g) all-purpose (plain) flour
1½	teaspoons baking powder
¼	cup (30 g) unsweetened cocoa powder
½	cup (50 g) unsweetened shredded (desiccated) coconut
½	cup (120 g) salted butter, softened
1	cup (200 g) sugar
½	teaspoon coconut extract (essence)
2	large eggs
1	cup (250 ml) milk

Chocolate Ganache

7	ounces (200 g) dark chocolate, chopped
¾	cup (180 g) salted butter, chopped

Cake: Preheat the oven to 350°F (180°C/gas 4). Grease an 8-inch (20-cm) springform pan. Line the base with parchment paper.

Sift the flour, baking powder, and cocoa into a bowl. Stir in the coconut.

Beat the butter, sugar, and coconut extract in a bowl with an electric mixer on medium-high speed until pale and creamy. Add the eggs one at a time, beating until just combined after each addition.

With the mixer on low speed, gradually beat in the flour mixture, alternating with the milk. Spoon the batter into the prepared pan, smoothing the top with the back of the spoon.

Bake for 50–55 minutes, until a toothpick inserted into the center comes out clean. Let cool in the pan for 10 minutes, then turn out onto a wire rack and let cool completely, about 1 hour.

Chocolate Ganache: Combine the chocolate and butter in a double boiler over barely simmering water. Stir until smooth. Remove from the heat and let cool to room temperature.

Beat the mixture with a wooden spoon until thick and spreadable.

Use a long serrated knife to cut the cake in half horizontally. Place the bottom half on a serving plate. Spread with one-third of the ganache. Place the remaining layer of cake on top and spread the top and sides with the remaining ganache. Slice and serve.

. . .

*If you liked this recipe,
you will love these as well.*

WHITE CHOCOLATE CHIP
COOKIES WITH COCONUT

COCONUT FUDGE
BROWNIES

COCONUT TRUFFLES

Serves: 12–15

Preparation: 20 minutes
+ 1½ hours to cool
& set

Cooking: 1 hour

Level: 2

· · · · ·

This is a very rich cake. Serve in tiny slivers with small cups of strong black coffee.

CHOCOLATE MUD CAKE

Cake

1¼	pounds (600 g) dark chocolate, coarsely chopped
1½	cups (375 g) salted butter, chopped
1	cup (250 ml) water
1	cup (200 g) firmly packed dark brown sugar
2	cups (300 g) all-purpose (plain) flour
½	teaspoon baking powder
4	large eggs, lightly beaten
⅓	cup (90 ml) dry Marsala wine

Glaze

5	ounces (150 g) dark chocolate, coarsely chopped
½	cup (120 ml) heavy (double) cream
1	tablespoon unsalted butter
1	tablespoon liquid glucose

Cake: Preheat the oven to 325°F (170°C/gas 3). Grease a 9-inch (23-cm) springform pan. Line the base with parchment paper.

Combine the chocolate, butter, water, and brown sugar in a heavy-based pan over low heat. Stir until melted and the sugar has dissolved. Set aside to cool for 30 minutes.

Add the flour, baking powder, eggs, and Marsala, stirring until just combined. Spoon the batter into the prepared pan.

Bake for 1 hour, until a toothpick inserted into the center comes out clean. Let the cake cool completely in the pan on a wire rack, about 1 hour.

Glaze: Combine the chocolate, cream, butter, and liquid glucose in a heavy-based saucepan over very low heat, stirring until melted. Let cool for 15 minutes.

Spoon the glaze over the cake. Let stand until set before serving, about 15 minutes.

· · ·

If you liked this recipe. you will love these as well.

MINI CHOCOLATE MUD CAKES

CHOCOLATE MINT TRUFFLE CAKE

FROZEN MISSISSIPPI MUD PIE

. . . . .

This tall, handsome cake will make a splash whenever you serve it.

DEVIL'S FOOD CAKE

Cake

3/4	cup (120 g) unsweetened cocoa powder
1/2	cup (120 ml) boiling water
3	cups (450 g) all-purpose (plain) flour
1	teaspoon baking soda (bicarbonate of soda)
1/2	teaspoon salt
1 1/2	cups (370 g) unsalted butter
2 1/4	cups (450 g) sugar
1	tablespoon vanilla extract (essence)
4	large eggs
1	cup (250 ml) milk

Frosting

1 1/2	pounds (750 g) dark chocolate, chopped
4	cups (1 liter) heavy (double) cream
1	teaspoon light corn (golden) syrup
	Shards and curls of milk and white chocolate, to decorate (optional)

Cake: Preheat the oven to 350°F (180°C/gas 4). Butter three 8-inch (20-cm) round cake pans. Line the bases with parchment paper. Dust the bottoms and sides of the pans with extra cocoa.

Sift the cocoa into a medium bowl and whisk in the boiling water. Set aside to cool. Sift the flour, baking soda, and salt into a large bowl.

Beat the butter and sugar in a bowl with an electric beater on medium-high speed until pale and creamy. Beat in the vanilla. Add the eggs one at a time, beating until just combined after each addition.

Whisk the milk into the reserved cocoa mixture. With the mixer on low speed, gradually beat the flour and cocoa mixtures into the batter.

Divide the batter evenly among the three prepared pans.

Bake for 35–45 minutes, until a toothpick inserted into the center of each layer comes out clean.

Transfer the pans to wire racks and let cool for 15 minutes. Turn the cakes out of the pans, and return to the racks, tops up, until completely cool.

Frosting: Place the chocolate and cream in a heavy-based saucepan over very low heat, stirring constantly, until smooth. Increase the heat to medium-low; cook, stirring, for 3 minutes more. Remove from the heat.

Stir in the corn syrup. Transfer the frosting to a large metal bowl. Chill until cool enough to spread, about 2 hours.

Remove the parchment from the bottoms of the cakes. Place one cake layer on a serving platter. Spread with 1 1/2 cups of chocolate frosting. Add the second cake layer, and spread with another 1 1/2 cups of frosting. Top with the third cake layer. Spread the top and sides of the cake with the remaining frosting.

Decorate with the shards and curls of milk and white chocolate, if using. Slice and serve.

Serves: 10–12
Preparation: 45 minutes
  + 2 hours to chill
Cooking: 45–50 minutes
Level: 2

CHOCOLATE MINT TRUFFLE CAKE

Cake

5   ounces (150 g) dark chocolate, chopped

2/3 cup (150 g) butter, chopped

3/4 cup (150 g) firmly packed light brown sugar

1/2 cup (120 ml) cold water

2   large eggs, lightly beaten

1 2/3 cups (250 g) all-purpose (plain) flour

2   teaspoons baking powder

2   tablespoons unsweetened cocoa powder

Chocolate Ganache

8   ounces (250 g) dark chocolate, chopped

2/3 cup (150 ml) heavy (double) cream

3   ounces (90 g) peppermint chocolate, finely chopped

Cake: Preheat the oven to 325°F (170°C/gas 3). Grease an 8-inch (20-cm) springform pan. Line the base with parchment paper.

Combine the chocolate, butter, brown sugar, and water in a saucepan over low heat. Cook and stir until melted and smooth. Set aside to cool for 15 minutes.

Add the eggs to the pan, stirring to combine. Sift in the flour, baking powder, and cocoa, stirring to combine. Spoon the batter into the prepared pan, smoothing the top with the back of the spoon.

Bake for 45–50 minutes, until a toothpick inserted into the center comes out clean. Let cool in the pan for 10 minutes, then turn out onto a wire rack and let cool completely.

Chocolate Ganache: Melt the chocolate and cream in a double boiler over barely simmering water, or in the microwave. Let cool for 5 minutes.

Divide the mixture evenly between two bowls. Chill one bowl for 2 hours, until firm. Leave the remaining bowl at room temperature for about 2 hours, until thick enough to spread. Spread the room temperature ganache over the top and sides of the cake.

Roll heaped teaspoons of the chilled ganache into 12 round truffles. Roll in the chopped peppermint chocolate. Arrange on top of the cake. Slice and serve.

. . .

If you liked this recipe, you will love these as well.

CHOCOLATE MINT CREAMS

CHOCOLATE MINT BARS

CHOCOLATE MINT HEARTS

Serves: 12–15

Preparation: 30 minutes
+ 5 hours to freeze
& soften

Cooking: 12 minutes

Level: 1

CHOCOLATE BIRTHDAY CAKE

Chocolate Cake

1	pound (500 g) dark chocolate, chopped
½	cup (120 g) unsalted butter, chopped
¼	cup (50 g) superfine (caster) sugar
4	large eggs
1	tablespoon all-purpose (plain) flour

Chocolate Ganache

¾	cup (180 ml) heavy (double) cream
8	ounces (250 g) dark chocolate, chopped

Chocolate Cake: Preheat the oven to 400°F (200°C/gas 6). Grease an 8-inch (20-cm) springform pan. Line the base with parchment paper.

Melt the chocolate, butter, and 1 tablespoon of sugar in a double boiler over barely simmering water. Set aside to cool slightly.

Beat the eggs and remaining sugar in a bowl with an electric mixer on medium speed until very thick and pale. Gently fold in the flour, followed by the chocolate mixture. Spoon the batter into the prepared pan, smoothing the top carefully with the back of the spoon.

Bake for 12 minutes. The cake will not be fully cooked or set. Remove from the oven and run a knife around the edges. Let cool in the pan, then place in the freezer for 4 hours, until firm.

Remove the cake from the freezer 1 hour before serving and leave at room temperature to soften.

Chocolate Ganache: Put the cream in a small saucepan over medium heat and bring almost to a boil. Put the chocolate in a heatproof bowl and pour in the hot cream. Stir until melted and smooth. Let cool for 15 minutes.

Pour the ganache over the cake. Slice and serve.

. . .

If you liked this recipe,
you will love these as well.

FROSTED MOCHA CAKE

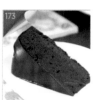

CHOCOLATE MUD CAKE

SACHERTORTE

Serves: 10–12
Preparation: 1 hour
Cooking: 10–14 minutes
Level: 3

· · · · ·

You will need five 8-inch (20-cm) cake pans to make this stunning cake. It dates back to the 19th century when it was invented for Prince Esterházy, a wealthy royal diplomat of the Austro-Hungarian Empire.

ESTERHÁZY TORTE

Cake

8	large egg whites
1⅓	cups (200 g) confectioners' (icing) sugar
1½	teaspoons finely grated unwaxed lemon zest
¼	teaspoon cinnamon
3	cups (300 g) finely ground almonds
¾	cup (120 g) all-purpose (plain) flour

Buttercream

1¼	cups (300 ml) milk
3½	ounces (100 g) dark chocolate, chopped
2	tablespoons cornstarch (cornflour)
2	large egg yolks
½	cup (50 g) sugar
2	tablespoons kirsch
1	cup (100 g) finely ground almonds
1	cup (250 g) butter
¾	cup (120 g) confectioners' (icing) sugar

Apricot Glaze

| 2 | tablespoons apricot preserves (jam) |
| 1 | teaspoon water |

Decoration

1½	cups (200 g) confectioners' (icing) sugar
2	tablespoons kirsch
2	ounces (60 g) dark chocolate, melted
4	tablespoons toasted flaked almonds

Cake: Preheat the oven to 350°F (180°C/gas 4). Cut out 5 parchment circles to fit 8-inch (20-cm) springform pans.

Beat the egg whites until soft peaks form. Gradually beat in the confectioners' sugar until stiff. Beat in the lemon zest and cinnamon. Fold the almonds and flour into the egg white mixture.

Divide the mixture evenly among the pans. Bake for 10–14 minutes until golden and pulling away from the sides. Put the baked cakes on their parchment paper on a flat surface to cool.

Buttercream: Heat ¾ cup (180 ml) of the milk in a small saucepan, add the chocolate, and stir until melted. Remove from the heat. Whisk the cornstarch in a bowl with the remaining milk, egg yolks, and sugar until smooth. Beat into the chocolate milk. Return the pan to the heat and whisk until it is thick and comes to a boil. Let bubble up just once, then remove from the heat. Whisk briskly, making sure no lumps form. Stir in the kirsch and almonds as it cools.

Beat the butter in a bowl until smooth. Gradually beat in the confectioners' sugar, followed by the chocolate mixture.

Peel the parchment paper off the cakes, reserving the best cake for the top. Sandwich four cake layers together with the buttercream. Spread the buttercream with a palette knife, reserving about half for the sides. Put the reserved cake on top.

Apricot Glaze: Mix the apricot preserves with the water, then strain. Brush the top cake and set aside.

Decoration: Mix the confectioners' sugar and kirsch in a small bowl. Spread over the top of the cake.

Spoon the melted dark chocolate into a pastry (piping) bag fitted with a small tip and pipe lines, about ¾ inch (2 cm) apart, across the frosting before it sets. Drag a toothpick through the lines in the opposite direction to make the pattern. Spread the sides of the cake with the reserved buttercream and sprinkle with the almonds, pressing lightly to make them stick to the frosting. Slice and serve.

Serves: 12
Preparation: 1 hour
  + 1 hour to set
Cooking: 6–8 minutes
Level: 3

. . . . .

This eight-layered chocolate buttercream cake (*Prinzregententorte*) was first made in 1886 for Luitpold, Prince Regent of Bavaria, and dedicated to him by his court confectioner. The layers symbolized the eight Bavarian governmental states.

The torte is made of eight separately baked cakes. Bake in 10-inch (26-cm) springform pans, without the rims.

PRINCE REGENT TORTE

Torte

6	large eggs, separated
1½	tablespoons hot water
1	cup (200 g) sugar
¼	teaspoon salt
1	teaspoon vanilla extract (essence)
1	teaspoon finely grated unwaxed lemon zest
⅓	cup (90 g) unsalted butter, melted
1	cup (150 g) all-purpose (plain) flour
3	tablespoons cornstarch (cornflour)
1	teaspoon baking powder

Filling

8	ounces (250 g) dark chocolate, chopped
½	cup (120 ml) milk
1	cup (250 g) unsalted butter
1⅔	cups (200 g) confectioners' (icing) sugar

Glaze

5	ounces (150 g) dark chocolate
1	tablespoon unsalted butter
12	walnut halves, to decorate

Torte: Preheat the oven to 350°F (180°C/gas 4). Butter the bases of eight 10-inch (26-cm) springform pans. Bake in batches if you don't have eight pans.

Beat the egg yolks and water in a large bowl with an electric mixer on high speed until frothy, 1–2 minutes. Whisk in two-thirds of the sugar and beat until pale and fluffy. Add the salt, vanilla, and lemon zest. Stir in the butter.

Beat the egg whites in a clean bowl with the mixer on high speed until soft peaks form. Add the remaining sugar and beat until stiff. Fold the egg white mixture into the yolk mixture.

Sift the flour, cornstarch, and baking powder into a bowl. Fold spoonfuls of the flour mixture into the egg mixture until combined. Spread each pan base with a very thin layer of batter, gently smoothing with the back of the spoon. Bake for 6–8 minutes, until pale golden brown. Let cool for a few minutes, then remove the cakes from the pan bases, and let cool completely on wire racks.

Filling: Put the chocolate in a heatproof bowl. Bring the milk to a boil in a small saucepan. Pour over the chocolate and stir until melted and cooled. Beat the butter and confectioners' sugar in a bowl with an electric mixer on medium speed until fluffy. Gradually fold in the chocolate mixture.

Reserve the best cake for the top. Place a cake on a serving plate and spread evenly with the chocolate cream. Cover with another cake and repeat until all the cakes are sandwiched together. Put the remaining cream in a pastry (piping) bag and chill with the cake while you make the glaze.

Glaze: Melt the chocolate and butter in a double boiler over barely simmering water until smooth and glossy. Pour over the cake while still warm. Spread thinly and evenly over the whole cake. Lightly score with 12 slices and decorate with walnut halves around the edges. Pipe the remaining cream around the bottom of the cake. Let set for at least 1 hour before serving.

Serves: 10–12

Preparation: 50 minutes
   + 5–6 hours to chill

Cooking: 50–60 minutes

Level: 3

· · · · ·

The Sachertorte is a famous Austrian chocolate cake, as served in the Hotel Sacher in Vienna. It was invented in 1832 by Franz Sacher for Prince Metternich. The original recipe is a closely guarded secret, so this is one of many adaptations. Only the Hotel Sacher serves the torte with its famous seal. It needs no decoration, though some confectioners pipe a large "S" on top. Serve with whipped cream.

SACHERTORTE

Torte

4	ounces (120 g) bittersweet chocolate, broken into pieces
2/3	cup (150 g) unsalted butter, softened
2/3	cup (100 g) confectioners' (icing) sugar
1/2	teaspoon vanilla bean paste
6	large eggs, separated
3/4	cup (125 g) all-purpose flour
1/2	cup (100 g) superfine (caster) sugar
2/3	cup (200 g) apricot preserves (jam)

Glaze

1	cup (200 g) sugar
1/2	cup (120 ml) water
5	ounces (150 g) bittersweet chocolate, broken into pieces

Torte: Preheat the oven to 325°F (170°C/gas 3). Line the base of a 10-inch (25-cm) springform pan with parchment paper. Brush the sides with melted butter and dust with flour.

Melt the chocolate in a double boiler over barely simmering water, or in the microwave. Set aside to cool a little.

Beat the butter and confectioners' sugar in a bowl with an electric mixer on medium-high speed until pale and creamy. Add the vanilla. Add the egg yolks one at a time, beating until just combined after each addition. Stir in the chocolate.

Beat the egg whites in a separate bowl with an electric mixer on medium speed, gradually adding the sugar until stiff and glossy. Spoon into the chocolate mixture and sift the flour over the top. Gently fold in with a large metal spoon. Spoon the batter into the prepared pan.

Bake for 50–60 minutes, until a toothpick inserted into the center comes out clean. Leave in the pan for 10 minutes, then turn the cake out onto a wire rack. Let cool for 20 minutes before peeling off the paper. Return upside down to the pan (to ensure an even shape), and let cool completely.

Slice the cake horizontally with a serrated knife. Warm the preserves, stir until smooth, and spread evenly on both cake halves. Sandwich the cake together again and brush all over with the remaining preserves.

Glaze: Bring the sugar and water to a boil in a small, heavy-based saucepan. Leave to bubble for 5–6 minutes, until the sugar has dissolved. Let cool a little.

Melting the chocolate in a double boiler over barely simmering water, or in the microwave. Beat into the sugar mixture until smooth and glossy. When the glaze has cooled to body temperature, pour over the cake in one sweeping movement, turning the plate as you do so. Touch the chocolate glaze as briefly as possible when spreading it around the sides with a palette knife, so that it remains glossy.

Chill for 5–6 hours before serving.

Serves: 10–12
Preparation: 45 minutes
    + 2¼ hours to cool
    & chill
Cooking: 30–35 minutes
Level: 3

BOSTON CREAM PIE

Cake

1   cup (150 g) all-purpose (plain) flour
¼   teaspoon salt
4   large eggs
1   cup (200 g) sugar
⅓   cup (90 ml) milk
1   vanilla bean, split lengthwise

Filling

6   large egg yolks
¾   cup (150 g) sugar
6½   tablespoons cornstarch (cornflour)
⅛   teaspoon salt
3   cups (750 ml) milk
2   teaspoons vanilla extract (essence)

Glaze

4   ounces (120 g) dark chocolate, coarsely chopped
½   cup (120 ml) heavy (double) cream
1   cup (150 g) confectioners' (icing) sugar
1   tablespoon boiling water

Cake: Preheat the oven to 350°F (180°C/gas 4). Line a 9-inch (23-cm) springform pan with parchment paper. Sift the flour and salt into a bowl.

Beat the eggs and sugar in a bowl with an electric mixer on medium speed until well combined. Place the bowl over a pan of gently simmering water and beat until the mixture is warm and the sugar is dissolved, 5–6 minutes. Remove from the heat. Beat again on high speed until thickened and pale, about 5 minutes.

Combine the milk and vanilla bean in a saucepan. Heat over medium heat; do not let it boil. Discard the vanilla bean. With the mixer on, pour the milk into the egg mixture in a slow, steady stream. Transfer to a bowl. Fold in the flour mixture. Spoon the batter into the prepared pan.

Bake for 30–35 minutes, until springy to the touch. Transfer to a wire rack and let cool for 15 minutes. Turn out onto the rack and let cool completely, about 1 hour.

Filling: Prepare an ice-water bath. Beat the egg yolks in a bowl. Put the sugar, cornstarch, and salt in a saucepan. Stir in the milk. Cook over medium heat, stirring constantly, until thickened. Remove from the heat.

Whisking constantly, slowly pour the hot milk mixture into the egg yolks. Return to the pan. Cook over medium heat, stirring constantly, until it begins to bubble. Remove from the heat and stir in the vanilla. Transfer to a bowl. Put the bowl in the ice bath. Stir from time to time until cool and thickened. Cover with plastic wrap (cling film).

Cut the cake in half horizontally with a serrated knife. Spread one half with the filling. Cover with the other layer. Chill until set, 30 minutes.

Glaze: Melt the chocolate and cream in a double boiler over barely simmering water. Put the cake on a serving plate. Pour the glaze over the top. Let set for 30 minutes.

Put the confectioners' sugar in a bowl with enough boiling water to make a thick glaze. Place in a plastic food bag and snip off one corner. Pipe thin circles of frosting on top of the cake. Use a toothpick to pull the white frosting downward. Slice and serve.

Serves: 8

Preparation: 2 hours
+ 1–2 hours to cool
& chill

Cooking: 6–10 minutes

Level: 3

. . . . .

The Dobos torte, or *Dobosh*, to give it its native Hungarian name, became famous in Budapest in 1885 when the chef Jozsef Dobos served it to Franz Joseph 1, Emperor of the Austro-Hungarian Empire. The cake quickly became popular all over Europe.

DOBOS TORTE

Cake

6	large eggs, separated
1	cup (150 g) confectioners' (icing) sugar
1	teaspoon finely grated unwaxed lemon zest
1	teaspoon vanilla extract (essence)
3/4	cup (120 g) all-purpose (plain) flour

Chocolate Buttercream

1	cup (250 g) unsalted butter, softened
2 2/3	cups (400 g) confectioners' (icing) sugar
1/2	cup (75 g) unsweetened cocoa powder
3–4	tablespoons milk
1	teaspoon vanilla extract (essence)

Caramel Glaze

1	cup (150 g) confectioners' (icing) sugar
1/2	tablespoon unsalted butter

Cake: Preheat the oven to 400°F (200°C/gas 6). Oil six non-stick baking sheets and line with parchment paper. Draw a circle around a 9-inch (23-cm) cake pan on each piece of paper.

Beat the egg yolks, half the confectioners' sugar, lemon zest, and vanilla in a bowl with an electric mixer on high speed until pale and thick.

Beat the egg whites in a bowl until soft peaks form. Gradually add the remaining confectioners' sugar, beating until stiff and glossy. Fold the egg white mixture into the egg yolk mixture, alternating with the flour.

Divide the batter evenly among the circles on the paper. Spread with a rubber spatula to fill the circles. Bake for 6–10 minutes, until golden and the tops are not sticky when touched. Let cool for 5 minutes, remove on their parchment from the sheets, and weigh down lightly with plates.

Chocolate Buttercream: Beat the butter in a bowl with an electric mixer on medium speed until pale. Gradually beat in the confectioners' sugar and cocoa. With the mixer on low speed, gradually beat in the milk and vanilla. Beat until fluffy, light, and airy.

When the cakes are completely cool, carefully peel off the paper and assemble the torte. Cut around the sponge circles with a knife, using the springform ring as a guide so they will stack up evenly. Reserve the best cake for the top.

Sandwich five cake layers together with the chocolate buttercream. Spread the remaining buttercream over the top and sides.

Caramel Glaze: Place the reserved cake layer on a board. Heat the confectioners' sugar in a small saucepan over low heat until golden. Add the butter and stir until smooth. Pour over the cake in one go, spreading with the back of a large spoon. Leave to cool and harden for 5–10 minutes.

Cut the glazed top with a long buttered knife into eight even wedges. Pull the knife through some butter before each new cut. Arrange the caramel-covered wedges on top of the torte and chill again until completely set, 1–2 hours.

Serves: 12
Preparation: 1 hour
  + 2 hours to chill
Cooking: 40–45 minutes
Level: 3

The Red Velvet Cake is believed to be a recipe from the southern United States, but it was made popular in the 1920s by the famous Waldorf-Astoria Hotel, in New York.

RED VELVET CAKE

Cake

3	cups (450 g) all-purpose (plain) flour
1/2	cup (75 g) unsweetened cocoa powder
1 1/2	teaspoons baking powder
1 1/2	teaspoons baking soda (bicarbonate of soda)
1	cup (250 g) salted butter, softened
2 1/4	cups (450 g) firmly packed light brown sugar
3	tablespoons red food coloring
2 1/2	teaspoons vanilla extract (essence)
3	large eggs
1 3/4	cups (430 ml) milk

Frosting

1 1/4	pounds (650 g) cream cheese, softened
1 1/4	cups (300 g) salted butter, softened
2	teaspoons vanilla extract (essence)
7	cups (1 kg) confectioners' (icing) sugar

Cake: Preheat the oven to 350°F (180°C/gas 4). Grease two deep 9-inch (23-cm) cake pans. Add 2 tablespoons of flour to each pan and shake to coat the bottom and sides.

Sift the flour, cocoa, baking powder, and baking soda into a bowl. Beat the butter with the brown sugar, food coloring, and vanilla in a large bowl with an electric mixer on medium-high speed until creamy. Add the eggs one at a time, beating until just combined after each addition. With the mixer on low speed, gradually beat in the flour mixture and milk. Spoon the batter into the prepared pans.

Bake for 40–45 minutes, until a toothpick inserted into the centers comes out clean. Cool in the pans for 15 minutes. Turn out onto a rack and let cool completely.

Frosting: Beat the cream cheese, butter, and vanilla in a large bowl until pale and creamy. Gradually beat in the confectioners' sugar.

Slice the rounded tops off the cakes. Crumble the trimmings into a bowl and set aside.

Slice each cake in half horizontally. Place one layer on a serving plate. Spread with 3/4 cup of the frosting. Repeat with the remaining three layers of cake and frosting.

Spread the remaining frosting over the top and sides of the cake. Gently press the reserved crumbs into the sides until evenly coated.

Chill for 2 hours before serving.

• • •

If you liked this recipe, you will love these as well.

RED VELVET CUPCAKES

CHOCOLATE CAKE WITH BEETS

FROSTED MOCHA CAKE

Serves: 12
Preparation: 1 hour
+ 5–12 hours to soak
& 2–3 to chill
Cooking: 30–35 minutes
Level: 3

CHOCOLATE CHERRY TORTE

Decoration

1	(15-ounce/450-g) can or jar of pitted cherries, drained
2	tablespoons kirsch
1–2	tablespoons unsweetened cocoa powder, to dust

Torte

12	ounces (350 g) bittersweet chocolate, coarsely chopped
1/2	cup (120 g) unsalted butter, softened
1	tablespoon kirsch
1/3	cup (50 g) all-purpose (plain) flour
3/4	cup (125 g) confectioners' (icing) sugar
1/2	cup (50 g) finely ground almonds
3	large eggs, separated
1³⁄₄	cups (450 ml) heavy (double) cream

Decoration: Soak the cherries with the kirsch in a bowl. Cover and leave for 5 hours, or overnight.

Torte: Preheat the oven to 325°F (170°C/gas 3). Line a 9-inch (23-cm) springform pan with parchment paper and butter the sides.

Melt 5 ounces (150 g) of the chocolate with the butter in a double boiler over barely simmering water. Remove from the heat, stir in the kirsch, and set aside cool slightly.

Sift the flour and confectioners' sugar into a bowl, then stir into the chocolate mixture. Add the almonds and egg yolks, beating until combined.

Beat the egg whites in a separate bowl until soft peaks form. Fold the egg whites into the chocolate mixture with a metal spoon. Spoon the batter evenly into the prepared pan.

Bake for 30–35 minutes, until a toothpick inserted in the center comes out clean. Cool in the pan for 10 minutes and then turn out onto a wire rack to cool completely.

Meanwhile, put the remaining 7 ounces (200 g) of bittersweet chocolate in a large heatproof bowl. Bring the cream to a boil in a saucepan over medium heat, then pour over the chocolate. Leave for a few minutes, then stir gently until smooth. When cooled, beat until thick and creamy.

Peel the parchment paper off the cake and return it to the cleaned cake pan. Spoon most of the cherries and their juices over the top. Spread with the chocolate cream and top with the remaining cherries. Chill for 2–3 hours, until set.

Remove the cake from the refrigerator and dust with the cocoa. Slice and serve.

Serves: 8
Preparation: 30 minutes
+ 1 hour to cool
& chill
Cooking: 12–15 minutes
Level: 2

CHOCOLATE BANANA ROULADE
with honeycomb chocolate

Roulade

4	ounces (120 g) dark chocolate, chopped
6	large eggs, separated
1/2	cup (100 g) superfine (caster) sugar
1/4	cup (30 g) unsweetened cocoa powder + extra, to dust
2	tablespoons potato starch (flour) or cornstarch (cornflour)
2	tablespoons boiling water

Filling

1	cup (250 g) mascarpone
2/3	cup (150 ml) dulce de leche
3	small honeycomb chocolate bars, coarsely chopped
1	small, just-ripe banana, diced

Roulade: Preheat the oven to 350°F (180°C/gas 4). Butter a 10 x 15-inch (25 x 35-cm) jelly-roll pan. Line with parchment paper.

Melt the chocolate in a double boiler over barely simmering water, or in the microwave. Set aside to cool.

Beat the egg yolks and sugar in a bowl with an electric mixer on high speed until thick and pale. Sift in the cocoa and potato starch, stirring in gently. Add the chocolate and boiling water, and stir gently to combine.

Beat the egg whites with an electric mixer on medium speed until soft peaks form. Fold into the chocolate mixture. Spoon the batter into the prepared pan.

Bake for 12–15 minutes, until springy to the touch. Dust generously with cocoa, then cover with a sheet of parchment paper. Invert the cake with the parchment paper onto a work surface.

While the cake is still hot, use the parchment paper to gently roll it up from one short side, rolling the paper with the cake. Let cool for 30 minutes.

Filling: Stir the mascarpone, dulce de leche, 2 honeycomb chocolate bars, and the banana in a bowl until partially combined.

Carefully unroll the cake and spread with the filling, leaving a 1-inch (2.5-cm) border all around. Reroll the cake. Cover and chill for 30 minutes.

Dust with extra cocoa and sprinkle with the remaining chopped honeycomb chocolate bar. Slice and serve.

. . .

If you liked this recipe, you will love these as well.

CHOCOLATE YULE LOG

CHOCOLATE ROLL WITH BOOZY BERRIES

CHOCOLATE HOKEY POKEY

. . . . .

A yule log is a large piece of wood that is traditionally burned in the hearth at Christmas time. This cake is named for the log. Serve it on Christmas Eve.

CHOCOLATE YULE LOG

Yule Log

2/3 cup (100 g) all-purpose (plain) flour

1/4 cup (30 g) unsweetened cocoa powder

1   teaspoon baking powder

5   large eggs, separated

3/4 cup (150 g) firmly packed light brown sugar

2   tablespoons water

    Superfine (caster) sugar, to sprinkle

Filling & Frosting

1   cup (250 ml) heavy (double) cream

15 ounces (450 g) dark chocolate, chopped

    Holly decorations

Yule Log: Preheat the oven to 350°F (180°C/gas 4). Butter a 10 x 15-inch (25 x 35-cm) jelly-roll pan. Line with parchment paper.

Sift the flour, cocoa, and baking powder into a bowl.

Beat the egg yolks, brown sugar, and water in a bowl with an electric mixer on medium speed until light in color and thick enough to leave a trail when the whisk blades are lifted. Fold in the flour mixture using a large metal spoon.

Beat the egg whites in a separate bowl until stiff. Fold into the batter using a large, clean metal spoon.

Spoon the batter evenly into the prepared pan. Bake for 10–12 minutes, until springy to the touch.

Put a large sheet of baking parchment on a work surface and sprinkle with superfine sugar. Turn the cake out onto the parchment and peel off the lining paper. Cover with a clean cloth. Let cool completely.

Trim the edges. Roll the cake up from one of the long sides, using the paper to help you, rolling the paper inside the cake.

Filling & Frosting: Bring the cream to a boil in a small pan, remove from the heat, then add 14 ounces (400 g) of the chocolate. Stir until melted and smooth. Leave to cool, then chill until spreadable, about 1 hour.

Grate the remaining chocolate. Spoon a third of the frosting into a bowl, and stir in the chocolate to make the filling.

Carefully unroll the cake, and spread with the filling, leaving a 1-inch (2.5-cm) border at the edges. Roll up the cake again using the paper as a guide. Set, seamside down, on a board.

Cut a thick diagonal slice off one end of the cake. Transfer the larger piece of cake to a board or flat serving plate. Spread a little frosting over the cut side of the small piece of cake and fix it to the large roll to make a branch. Spread the remaining frosting over the cake. Decorate with the holly. Slice and serve.

Serves: 6–8
Preparation: 30 minutes
  + 3 hours to
  macerate
Cooking: 10–12 minutes
Level: 2

CHOCOLATE ROLL
with boozy berries

Boozy Berries
3   cups (450 g) strawberries, hulled, halved
1/4 cup (60 ml) orange liqueur
2   tablespoons superfine (caster) sugar

Chocolate Roll
6   large eggs, separated
1/2 cup (100 g) superfine (caster) sugar
1/4 cup (30 g) unsweetened cocoa powder
2   tablespoons all-purpose (plain) flour
3 1/2 ounces (100 g) dark chocolate, melted, cooled
2   tablespoons milk

Filling
1 1/4 cups (300 ml) heavy (double) cream
     Unsweetened cocoa powder, to dust

Boozy Berries: Combine the strawberries, orange liqueur, and sugar in a bowl. Set aside for 3 hours to macerate.

Chocolate Roll: Preheat the oven to 350°F (180°C/gas 4). Brush a 10 x 12-inch (30 x 24-cm) jelly-roll pan with melted butter. Line the base with parchment paper, leaving about 2 inches (5 cm) overhanging on the short sides.

Beat the egg yolks and sugar in a large bowl with an electric mixer on medium-high speed until pale and thick. Sift in the cocoa and flour, folding gently to combine. Add chocolate and milk, folding gently to combine.

Beat the egg whites in a separate bowl with the mixer on medium speed until soft peaks form. Fold one-quarter of the egg whites into the chocolate mixture. Fold in the remaining egg whites until just combined.

Spoon the batter into the prepared pan, smoothing the surface with the back of the spoon.

Bake for 10–12 minutes, until firm and springy to the touch. Carefully turn the cake out onto a sheet of parchment paper. Set aside for 5 minutes to cool.

Use a sharp knife to carefully trim the edges. Starting from the short side closest to you, and using the paper as a guide, gently roll up the cake. Set aside for 5 minutes to cool. Gently unroll the cake.

Filling: Beat the cream in a bowl until firm peaks form. Spread over the cake, leaving a 2-inch (5-cm) border at the short side furthest from you. Using the paper as a guide, roll up the cake. Dust with cocoa.

Slice and serve with the boozy strawberries spooned over the top.

Serves: 8
Preparation: 30 minutes
  + 1½–2½ hours to
  chill
Cooking: 8–10 minutes
Level: 2

CELEBRATION ROLL

Roll

4	large eggs, separated
½	cup (100 g) superfine (caster) sugar + extra, to sprinkle
2	tablespoons vanilla sugar
¾	cup (125 g) all-purpose (plain) flour
2	teaspoons baking powder
1	tablespoon unsweetened cocoa powder
⅛	teaspoon salt

Filling

¾	cup (180 ml) heavy (double) cream
½	cup (75 g) toasted hazelnuts, finely chopped

Glaze

7	ounces (200 g) dark chocolate
¾	cup (150 g) firmly packed light brown sugar
5	tablespoons water
	Confectioners' (icing) sugar, to dust

Roll: Preheat the oven to 350°F (180°C/gas 4). Line a 9 x 13-inch (23 x 33-cm) jelly-roll pan with parchment paper.

Beat the egg yolks and both sugars in a large bowl with an electric mixer on medium speed until pale and thick. Sift in the flour, baking powder, cocoa, and salt, folding gently to combine.

Beat the egg whites and salt in a separate bowl until stiff peaks form. Fold a spoonful of the egg whites into the batter, then fold in the rest. Spoon the batter evenly into the prepared pan.

Bake for 8–10 minutes, until firm to the touch. Turn the cake out onto a clean damp kitchen cloth sprinkled with superfine sugar. Peel off the paper, trim the ends, and roll up loosely into a log from one short side, using the cloth as a guide. Leave to cool.

Filling: Beat the cream until it stands in soft peaks. Stir in the nuts.

Carefully unroll the log and spread with the cream mixture, leaving a 1-inch (2.5-cm) border around the edges. Roll up again. Wrap in parchment paper and chill for 30 minutes.

Glaze: Melt the chocolate with the brown sugar and water in a small heavy-based saucepan over low heat, stirring until smooth. Bring to a gentle boil and simmer for 2 minutes, stirring all the time, until the sugar has completely dissolved. Let cool.

Take the roll out of the refrigerator, remove the parchment paper, and place on a wire rack with a baking sheet underneath. Spread the glaze over the cake.

Place on a serving dish and dust with confectioners' sugar. Chill for 1–2 hours. Slice and serve.

pastries, tarts & pies

Based on shortcrust, puff, or choux pastry,
the recipes in this chapter include
mouthwatering turnovers, galettes, strudels,
cream puffs, tarts, and pies.

Serves: 4–6
Preparation: 15 minutes
Cooking: 20–25 minutes
Level: 1

. . . . .

A jalousie is a light French fruit-filled pastry dessert.
It falls somewhere between a turnover and a strudel.

CHOCOLATE PEAR JALOUSIE

$1/2$ cup (50 g) finely ground almonds

$1/4$ cup (50 g) firmly packed dark brown sugar

$3^1/2$ ounces (100 g) dark chocolate, grated

1 (8-ounce/250-g) sheet ready-rolled puff pastry

1 (14-ounce/400-g) can pear halves in juice, drained and thinly sliced

1 large egg white, lightly beaten

1 tablespoon raw sugar

Fresh cream, to serve (optional)

Preheat the oven to 400°F (200°C/gas 6). Line a baking sheet with parchment paper.

Combine the almonds, brown sugar, and chocolate in a bowl.

Cut the pastry sheet in half lengthwise. Place one piece of pastry on the prepared baking sheet. Sprinkle with the almond mixture, leaving a 1-inch (2.5-cm) border all around the edges. Top with the slices of pear.

Use a rolling pin to roll the other piece of pastry to make it about $1/2$ inch (1 cm) longer and wider. Fold the pastry in half lengthwise. Use a knife to cut slits into the folded edge, about $3/4$ inch (2 cm) apart, leaving a $3/4$-inch (2-cm) border on each side and the bottom, unfolded edge. Unfold the pastry and place over the pears, pressing the edges with a fork to seal.

Brush with the egg white and sprinkle with the raw sugar.

Bake for 20–25 minutes, until the pastry is puffed and golden. Serve warm or at room temperature, with the cream, if desired.

. . .

If you liked this recipe, you will love these as well.

CHOCOLATE CHERRY
TURNOVERS

CHOCOLATE PEAR
GALETTES

CHOCOLATE & RICOTTA
JALOUSIE

CHOCOLATE CHERRY TURNOVERS

6 ounces (180 g) dark chocolate, chopped

12 large marshmallows, coarsely chopped

1/4 cup (30 g) chopped candied (glacé) cherries

1/2 cup (50 g) shredded (desiccated) coconut

2 large egg whites

2 (8-ounce/250-g) sheets ready-rolled puff pastry

Preheat the oven to 375°F (190°C/gas 5). Line two baking sheets with parchment paper.

Combine the chocolate, marshmallows, cherries, and coconut in a large bowl. Add the egg whites and mix until well combined. Set aside.

Using a round 4-inch (10-cm) cookie cutter, cut out 12 disks from the pastry sheets. Place a spoonful of the chocolate mixture on half the disks, leaving a 1/2-inch (1-cm) border around the edges.

Cover with the remaining disks of the pastry. Use a fork to seal the edges. Place on the prepared baking sheets.

Bake for 15 minutes, until golden. Serve warm or at room temperature.

Serves: 6 Preparation: 15 minutes Cooking: 15 minutes Level: 1

EASY PAN AU CHOCOLAT

2 (8-ounce/250-g) sheets ready-rolled puff pastry

8 tablespoons chocolate hazelnut spread (Nutella)

1 large egg, lightly beaten

Preheat the oven to 350°F (180°C/gas 4). Line a large baking sheet with parchment paper.

Cut each sheet of pastry into four squares. Spread 1 tablespoon of chocolate hazelnut spread over each square, leaving a 1/2-inch (1-cm) border all around the edges.

Brush the edges of the pastry lightly with egg. Roll up each square from corner to corner, pressing gently to seal. Stretch the ends of the pastry rolls a little to form into half-moon shapes. Place on the prepared baking sheet. Brush with the egg.

Bake for 20–25 minutes, until the pastry is golden and puffed. Serve warm.

Serves: 4 Preparation: 15 minutes Cooking: 20–25 minutes Level: 1

You could also make these turnovers using fresh or canned cherries. Omit the marshmallows and candied (glacé) cherries, and replace with 1 cup of pitted and chopped fresh or canned cherries. If using canned fruit, make sure it is well drained.

Serve these simple chocolate treats warm for a special breakfast or brunch. They go beautifully with coffee.

Serves: 4
Preparation: 20 minutes
Cooking: 15 minutes
Level: 1

. . . . .

Galette is a French term for a crusty cake. It can be sweet or savory, and is usually based on pastry.

CHOCOLATE PEAR GALETTES

1   (8-ounce/250-g) sheet ready-rolled puff pastry, quartered
2   ounces (60 g) plain chocolate cookies
¼   cup (60 g) salted butter, chopped
¼   cup (50 g) superfine (caster) sugar
1   (14-ounce/400-g) can pear halves in juice, drained (reserving ¼ cup /60 ml juice), thinly sliced

Preheat the oven to 400°F (200°C/gas 6). Grease a baking sheet and line with parchment paper. Place the pastry on the prepared baking sheet.

Chop the cookies, butter, and sugar in a food processor or mix in a bowl with a fork until well combined. Divide the mixture evenly among the pastry squares, leaving a ½-inch (1-cm) border round the edges.

Arrange the pears over the cookie mixture. Brush the pastry with the reserved juice. Bake for 20–25 minutes, until puffed and golden. Serve warm.

. . .

If you liked this recipe, you will love these as well.

CHOCOLATE PEAR JALOUSIE

CHOCOLATE CHERRY TURNOVERS

INNSBRUCK CHOCOLATE NUT STRUDEL

Serves: 6
Preparation: 30 minutes
Cooking: 40–45 minutes
Level: 2

. . . . .

This is a hearty strudel that can be served warm or at room temperature. It is delicious with whipped cream and chocolate sauce. Try it with our chocolate sauce recipe on page 220.

INNSBRUCK CHOCOLATE NUT STRUDEL

Filling

3 cups (300 g) hazelnuts

¼ cup (60 g) salted butter, melted

½ cup (100 g) sugar

½ teaspoon ground cinnamon

3 large eggs, separated

2 ounces (60 g) dark chocolate, grated or finely chopped

To Assemble

6 sheets phyllo (filo) pastry

⅓ cup (100 g) unsalted butter, melted

½ cup (50 g) finely chopped hazelnuts

⅓ cup (60 g) golden raisins (sultanas), soaked in rum

Filling: Preheat the oven to 350°F (180°C/gas 4). Line two baking sheets with parchment paper.

Place the hazelnuts on one of the baking sheets and bake for 6 minutes. Put the hot nuts on a clean kitchen cloth and rub the skins off. Finely chop or grind and set aside.

Beat the butter, sugar, and cinnamon in a bowl with an electric mixer on medium-high speed until pale and creamy. Add the egg yolks one at a time, beating until just combined after each addition. Stir in the nuts and chocolate by hand.

Beat the egg whites in a clean bowl until stiff. Fold into the nut and chocolate mixture until just combined.

To Assemble: Lay a sheet of phyllo pastry on a clean work surface, brush with melted butter, and sprinkle with nuts. Keep the remaining sheets of phyllo pastry covered with a damp cloth to stop them drying out. Repeat the layering, buttering, and sprinkling with the remaining five sheets of phyllo.

Spoon the filling along one long side of the phyllo and sprinkle with the golden raisins. Leave a 2½-inch (5-cm) border at both short ends. Fold the ends in and over the filling and gently roll up the strudel. Lift onto the remaining prepared baking sheet with a spatula. Brush with butter.

Bake for 35–40 minutes, until golden brown and crisp. Give the strudel another brushing of butter halfway through baking. Serve warm or at room temperature.

. . .

If you liked this recipe, you will love these as well.

CHOCOLATE CHERRY TURNOVERS

EASY PAN AU CHOCOLAT

CHOCOLATE & RICOTTA JALOUSIE

Serves: 4–6
Preparation: 20 minutes
    + 10 minutes to cool
Cooking: 20–25 minutes
Level: 2

CHOCOLATE & RICOTTA JALOUSIE

8   ounces (250 g) fresh
     ricotta, drained
1   large egg, separated
$\frac{1}{4}$ cup (50 g) superfine
     (caster) sugar + 1
     tablespoon extra, to
     sprinkle
2   ounces (60 g) dark
     chocolate, grated
$\frac{1}{4}$ cup (50 g) mixed
     candied (glacé) peel
2   tablespoons toasted
     slivered almonds
1   tablespoon brandy
1   (8-ounce/250-g)
     sheet ready-rolled
     puff pastry

Preheat the oven to 400°F (200°C/gas 6). Line a baking sheet with parchment paper.

Combine the ricotta, egg yolk, $\frac{1}{4}$ cup of sugar, chocolate, candied peel, almonds, and brandy in a medium bowl.

Cut the pastry sheet in half lengthwise. Place one piece of pastry on the prepared baking sheet. Spread the ricotta mixture over the pastry, leaving a 1-inch (2.5-cm) border all around the edges.

Use a rolling pin to roll the other piece of pastry out to about $\frac{1}{2}$ inch (1 cm) longer and wider. Fold the pastry in half lengthwise. Use a knife to cut slits into the folded edge, about $\frac{3}{4}$ inch (2 cm) apart, leaving a $\frac{3}{4}$-inch (2-cm) border on each side and the bottom, unfolded edge. Unfold the pastry and place over the ricotta mixture, pressing the edges to seal.

Bake for 20–25 minutes, until the pastry is puffed and golden. Let cool for 10 minutes before serving.

. . .

If you liked this recipe, you will love these as well.

CHOCOLATE PEAR JALOUSIE

EASY PAN AU CHOCOLAT

INNSBRUCK CHOCOLATE NUT STRUDEL

Serves: 4–6
Preparation: 45 minutes
    + 1 hour to chill
Cooking: 15–20 minutes
Level: 3

. . . . .

Cannoli are a traditional Sicilian dessert. You will need the freshest of ricotta cheese and six cannoli molds to prepare this recipe.

CHOCOLATE & VANILLA CANNOLI

Filling

14	ounces (400 g) fresh ricotta
1	cup (200 g) sugar
3/4	cup (75 g) mixed chopped candied (glacé) peel
2	tablespoons orange flower water or orange liqueur
2	ounces (60 g) dark chocolate, grated
1	tablespoon unsweetened cocoa powder

Pastry

1 2/3	cups (250 g) all-purpose (plain) flour
1	tablespoon sugar
1	tablespoon unsweetened cocoa powder
1/3	cup (90 ml) Marsala wine
1	teaspoon instant coffee
1/8	teaspoon salt
2	cups (500 ml) vegetable oil, for frying

To Decorate

	Candied peel
	Red and green candied (glacé) cherries
2	tablespoons confectioners' (icing) sugar

Filling: Press the ricotta through a fine-mesh sieve. Mix the ricotta, sugar, candied peel, orange flower water, and chocolate in a large bowl. Divide the mixture between two bowls. Add the cocoa to one of the bowls and mix well.

Pastry: Mix the flour, sugar, cocoa, Marsala, coffee, and salt in a large bowl to make a soft dough. Cover and chill in the refrigerator for 1 hour.

Roll out the dough on a lightly floured surface to 1/8 inch (3 mm) thick.

Cut into ovals large enough to wrap around the cannoli molds. Wrap an oval of pastry around each mold. Overlap the pastry where it meets and seal using a little of the egg white.

Heat the oil in a deep-fryer or deep saucepan to 365°F (185°C). If you don't have a frying thermometer, test the oil temperature by dropping a small piece of bread into the hot oil. If the bread immediately bubbles to the surface and begins to turn golden, the oil is ready.

Fry the pastry-coated tubes until the pastry is golden brown, 3–4 minutes. Drain on paper towels and let cool. Slip the pastry cases off the molds. Repeat until all the pastry is fried.

Fill the cooled cannoli with the plain ricotta mixture from one end and the chocolate ricotta mixture from the other end.

To Decorate: Press pieces of candied peel and cherries into the filling at the ends. Dust with confectioners' sugar and serve.

. . .

If you liked this recipe, you will love these as well.

CHOCOLATE & RICOTTA JALOUSIE

CHURROS WITH AZTEC SAUCE

RICOTTA CREAM PUFFS WITH CHOCOLATE FROSTING

Serves: 12
Preparation: 30 minutes
Cooking: 30 minutes
Level: 2

. . . . .

Churros are a mouthwatering Spanish dish that have become popular all over the world. Traditionally served for breakfast, they are good any time of the day. This recipe uses a chile-flavored chocolate for the sauce, but you could also use plain dark chocolate and chili powder.

CHURROS WITH AZTEC SAUCE

Churros

1¹/₃	cups (200 g) all-purpose (plain) flour
¹/₄	teaspoon salt
1¹/₄	cups (300 ml) water
²/₃	cup (150 g) unsalted butter
4	large eggs
4	cups (1 liter) vegetable oil, to deep-fry
¹/₂	cup (100 g) superfine (caster) sugar
2	teaspoons ground cinnamon

Aztec Sauce

4	cups (1 liter) milk
8	ounces (250 g) dark chile-flavored chocolate, coarsely chopped

Churros: Sift the flour and salt into a bowl.

Put the water and butter in a medium saucepan over low heat and cook, stirring with a wooden spoon, until the butter melts. Bring to a boil. Add the flour mixture and cook, stirring, until the mixture forms a ball and comes away from the side of the pan. Let cool for 5 minutes.

Add the eggs to the flour mixture one at a time, beating until well combined and the mixture is thick and glossy. Transfer to a pastry (piping) bag fitted with a ¹/₂-inch (1-cm) fluted nozzle.

Heat the oil in a deep-fryer or deep saucepan to 365°F (185°C). If you don't have a frying thermometer, test the oil temperature by dropping a small piece of bread into the hot oil. If the bread immediately bubbles to the surface and begins to turn golden, the oil is ready.

Pipe 4-inch (10-cm) lengths into the hot oil and fry until golden. Remove from the oil with tongs or a slotted spoon and drain on paper towels. Continue until all the dough is used. You should have 24 churros.

Combine the sugar and cinnamon on a large plate. Roll the warm churros in the cinnamon sugar to coat.

Aztec Sauce: Bring the milk to a boil in a medium saucepan over medium heat. Remove from heat and add the chocolate. Use a metal spoon to stir until melted and smooth. Divide the hot chile chocolate among serving bowls and serve hot with the churros.

. . .

If you liked this recipe, you will love these as well.

CHOCOLATE & RICOTTA JALOUSIE

CHOCOLATE & VANILLA CANNOLI

RICOTTA CREAM PUFFS WITH CHOCOLATE FROSTING

Serves: 6–8
Preparation: 30 minutes
    + 45 minutes to cool
    & set
Cooking: 30–35 minutes
Level: 3

· · · · ·

Cream puffs, also known as profiteroles, are made by filling balls of baked choux pastry with whipped cream, pastry cream, or ice cream.

RICOTTA CREAM PUFFS
with chocolate frosting

Choux Pastry

1	cup (250 ml) water
$1/3$	cup (90 g) salted butter, softened
1	cup (150 g) all-purpose (plain) flour
3	large eggs, lightly beaten

Filling

10	ounces (300 g) dark chocolate
14	ounces (400 g) fresh ricotta, drained
$1/2$	cup (75 g) dry-roasted hazelnuts, coarsely chopped
2	tablespoons confectioners' (icing) sugar
1	tablespoon finely grated unwaxed orange zest

Choux Pastry: Preheat the oven to 400°F (200°C/gas 6). Line two large baking sheets with parchment paper.

Combine the water and butter in a saucepan over medium heat and bring to a boil. Remove from the heat and use a wooden spoon to beat in the flour until combined.

Return to medium heat, stirring constantly, until the mixture forms a ball and comes away from the sides of the pan, 2–3 minutes. Set aside for 5 minutes to cool.

Gradually add the eggs, 1 tablespoon at a time, beating well after each addition, until the dough is thick and glossy.

Place heaped dessertspoons of the dough on the prepared baking sheets, spacing about 1 inch (2.5 cm) apart. Sprinkle the baking sheets with water to create steam.

Bake for 30–35 minutes, until puffed and golden. Turn off the oven. Use a knife to pierce the base of each cream puff. Return the cream puffs to the oven for 20 minutes to dry out. Transfer to a wire rack to cool.

Filling: Finely grate 2 ounces (60 g) of the chocolate. Stir the ricotta, grated chocolate, hazelnuts, confectioners' sugar, and orange zest in a bowl until well combined. Use a teaspoon to fill each cream puff with the ricotta mixture, pushing it in through the holes in the bottom.

Melt the remaining chocolate in a double boiler over barely simmering water, or in the microwave. Let cool a little.

Dip each cream puff into the chocolate. Let sit for 5 minutes, then dip into the chocolate again. Spoon any remaining chocolate over the cream puffs. Let sit for 15 minutes until set before serving.

Serves: 8

Preparation 45 minutes
    + 30 minutes to
    thicken & set

Cooking: 35–40 minutes

Level: 2

. . . . .

A croquembouche is a French dessert made up of a triangular stack of filled cream puffs (profiteroles) usually bathed in a chocolate sauce or finished with an elegant spun sugar decoration.

CHOCOLATE HAZELNUT CROQUEMBOUCHE

Cream Puffs

1   recipe choux pastry
    (see page 218)

Chocolate Sauce

$3^{1}/_{2}$ ounces (100 g) dark
    chocolate, chopped

$3^{1}/_{2}$ ounces (100 g) milk
    chocolate, chopped

$^{1}/_{3}$ cup (90 ml) heavy
    (double) cream

Filling

$^{1}/_{2}$ cup (120 ml) heavy
    (double) cream

$^{1}/_{2}$ cup (120 g)
    chocolate hazelnut
    spread (Nutella),
    warmed

$^{1}/_{3}$ cup (40 g) toasted
    hazelnuts, chopped

Cream Puffs: Prepare the cream puffs following the instructions on page 218. Set aside while you prepare the filling and sauce.

Chocolate Sauce: Combine both types of chocolate with the cream in a double boiler over barely simmering water, stirring until melted and smooth. Remove from the heat and set aside until the mixture has thickened, about 15 minutes.

Filling: Beat the cream in a bowl until thickened. Spoon into a pastry (piping) bag fitted with a $^{1}/_{2}$-inch (1-cm) plain nozzle. Pipe some cream into each cream puff, filling them about half full. Repeat with the hazelnut spread to fill.

Assemble the filled cream puffs in a triangular stack on a cake stand. Drizzle with the chocolate sauce. Sprinkle with the hazelnuts. Set aside for 15 minutes to set before serving.

. . .

If you liked this recipe,
you will love these as well.

RICOTTA CREAM PUFFS
WITH CHOCOLATE
FROSTING

MINI CROQUEMBOUCHES
WITH SUGAR NETTING

PARIS-BREST

Serves: 12
Preparation: 30 minutes
    + 1½ hours to cool
Cooking: 1 hour
Level: 3

. . . . .

The croquembouche dates back to medieval times but it was made popular by the famous French chef Anton Carème (1783–1833), as a special dessert for weddings, baptisms, and other family celebrations.

MINI CROQUEMBOUCHES
with sugar netting

Cream Puffs
1 recipe choux pastry (see page 218)
1 small egg, lightly beaten

Filling
1¼ cups (310 ml) heavy (double) cream
6 ounces (180 g) dark chocolate, melted and cooled

Sugar Netting
2 cups (400 g) superfine (caster) sugar
2 cups (500 ml) cold water

Cream Puffs: Prepare the cream puffs following the instructions on page 218. Set aside while you prepare the filling and sugar netting.

Filling: Beat the cream until soft peaks form. Gradually beat in the cooled chocolate until well combined.

Spoon the cream into a pastry (piping) bag fitted with a ¼-inch (5-mm) plain nozzle. Pipe the cream into the puffs.

Sugar Netting: Place the sugar and water in a heavy-based saucepan over medium heat. Stir, without boiling, for 5 minutes until the sugar is dissolved. Bring to a boil. Boil, without stirring, until golden, 18–20 minutes.

Arrange the cream puffs into 12 pyramid shapes on two baking sheets lined with parchment paper. Drizzle with a little of the sugar mixture to secure. Dip a fork into remaining sugar mixture. Drizzle thin strands around profiteroles.

Set aside for 10 minutes to set before transferring to plates to serve .

. . .

If you liked this recipe, you will love these as well.

RICOTTA CREAM PUFFS WITH CHOCOLATE FROSTING

CHOCOLATE HAZELNUT CROQUEMBOUCHE

PARIS-BREST

Serves: 8

Preparation: 45 minutes
  + 1¼ hours to set
  & chill

Cooking: 45–50 minutes

Level: 3

. . . . .

This is another famous French pastry. It was invented in 1891 to celebrate a bicycle race from Paris to Brest that still takes place once every four years. The round cake with a hole in the middle is meant to represent a bicycle wheel.

PARIS-BREST

³/₄ cup (180 ml) water

¹/₄ cup (60 g) salted butter, chopped

³/₄ cup (120 g) all-purpose (plain) flour

3 large eggs, lightly beaten

1 recipe vanilla custard (see page 285) or 2 cups (500 ml) fairly firm ready-made vanilla custard

1 cup (250 ml) heavy (double) cream

1 tablespoon confectioners' (icing) sugar

5 ounces (150 g) dark chocolate, coarsely chopped

2 tablespoons flaked almonds

Preheat the oven to 400°F (200°C/gas 6). Line a baking sheet with parchment paper. Draw an 8-inch (20-cm) disk on the paper.

Combine the water and butter in a saucepan over medium heat and bring to a boil. Remove from the heat and use a wooden spoon to beat in the flour until combined.

Return to medium heat, stirring constantly, until the mixture forms a ball and comes away from the sides of the pan, 2–3 minutes. Set aside for 5 minutes to cool. Gradually add the eggs, 1 tablespoon at a time, beating well after each addition, until the dough is thick and glossy.

Place tablespoons of the choux pastry around the disk drawn on the paper, leaving a hole in the center. Use a spatula to shape into a ring.

Bake for 40–45 minutes, until puffed and golden. Transfer to a wire rack and let cool completely.

Dry-fry the almonds in a frying pan over medium-low heat until toasted, 2–3 minutes. Set aside.

Use a serrated knife to cut the pastry ring in half horizontally. Discard any pieces of uncooked dough in the center. Place one piece cut-side up on a serving platter.

Put the custard in a pastry (piping) bag fitted with a ¹/₂-inch (1-cm) plain nozzle. Pipe over the pastry base.

Beat the cream and confectioners' sugar in a bowl until firm peaks form. Put the cream mixture in a clean pastry (piping) bag fitted with a ¹/₂-inch (1-cm) plain nozzle. Pipe over the custard. Top with the remaining pastry. Chill in the refrigerator for 1 hour.

Melt the chocolate in a double boiler over barely simmering water, stirring until smooth. Set aside to cool for 15 minutes, then drizzle over the pastry. Sprinkle with the almonds and serve.

Serves: 12
Preparation: 40 minutes
    + 30 minutes to chill,
    if required
Cooking: 15 minutes
Level: 2

. . . . .

You will need four 11-inch (28-cm) springform pans to bake the pastry for this torte. If you don't have four, bake the pastry bases one at a time, or in batches.

FRISIAN STREUSEL TORTE

Pastry

- 1²/₃ cups (250 g) all-purpose flour
- ¹/₂ teaspoon baking powder
- 3 tablespoons vanilla sugar
- ²/₃ cup (150 ml) crème fraîche
- ³/₄ cup (180 g) unsalted butter

Streusel

- 1¹/₄ cups (180 g) all-purpose (plain) flour
- ¹/₂ cup (100 g) firmly packed light brown sugar
- 1 teaspoon cocoa powder
- ¹/₂ cup (120 g) unsalted butter

Filling

- 2 cups (500 ml) heavy (double) cream
- 1 tablespoon vanilla sugar
- 2 teaspoons confectioners' (icing) sugar
- 1 (14-ounce/400-g) jar chocolate hazelnut spread (Nutella)

Pastry: Preheat the oven to 350°F (180°C/gas 4). Lightly oil four 11-inch (28-cm) springform pan bases.

Combine all the pastry ingredients in an electric mixer with a dough hook attachment and beat at high speed until combined. Transfer to a lightly floured work surface and knead into a smooth dough. If the dough is very sticky, chill for 30 minutes.

Divide the dough into four equal portions. Roll each piece out to fit one pan base. Place on the bases and prick with a fork. Clip the springform pan sides to the bases.

Streusel: Combine the flour, brown sugar, and cocoa in a bowl. Rub in the butter with your fingertips until crumbly. Sprinkle evenly over the pastry bases. Bake for about 15 minutes, until pale golden brown.

Release from the springform pans immediately and transfer to racks. Cut one of the four streusel bases into 12 slices and leave to cool on a wire rack with the others.

Filling: Beat the cream in a bowl until it stands in soft peaks. Add both sugars and beat until stiff.

When the streusel bases are completely cool, spread the three uncut bases with an even layer of chocolate hazelnut spread. Fill a pastry (piping) bag fitted with a star nozzle with the whipped cream and pipe one-third of the cream over the filling on the pastry bases.

Assemble into a torte and top with the 12 pre-cut streusel slices. Chill until ready to serve. Slice following the pre-cut slices.

. . .

If you liked this recipe, you will love these as well.

CHOCOLATE PEAR JALOUSIE

EASY PAN AU CHOCOLAT

INNSBRUCK CHOCOLATE NUT STRUDEL

Serves: 6
Preparation: 30 minutes
 + 2½ hours to chill
Cooking: 15–20 minutes
Level: 2

CHOCOLATE TARTLETS
with raspberries

Pastry

1	cup (150 g) all-purpose (plain) flour
⅓	cup (50 g) unsweetened cocoa powder
½	teaspoon baking powder
⅛	teaspoon salt
2	tablespoons sugar
⅓	cup (90 g) cold unsalted butter
3	tablespoons iced water

Filling

12	ounces (350 g) white chocolate, coarsely chopped
½	cup (120 ml) heavy (double) cream
2	large egg whites
4	tablespoons sugar
1	tablespoon Grand Marnier
1	cup (150 g) fresh raspberries

Pastry: Mix the flour, cocoa, baking powder, and salt in a large bowl. Stir in the sugar. Add the butter and mix gently with your fingertips until the mixture resembles a soft crumble. Stir enough water into the dough to form a ball.

Wrap the dough in plastic wrap (cling film) and chill in the refrigerator for at least 30 minutes.

Preheat the oven to 350°F (180°C/gas 4). Butter six 4-inch (10-cm) tartlet pans.

Roll the dough out on a lightly floured work surface. Cut into six disks and use them to line the prepared pans. Prick well with a fork.

Bake until the dough is golden, 15–20 minutes. Let cool on a rack.

Filling: Stir the white chocolate in a double boiler over barely simmering water until melted. Remove from the heat and let cool a little.

Stir the cream into the melted chocolate. Let cool to room temperature, then chill in the refrigerator for 2 hours.

Place the egg whites and sugar in a double boiler over barely simmering water and whisk until the sugar is melted. Remove from the heat and beat until the mixture is cool and the whites have thickened.

Stir the Grand Marnier into the chocolate mixture. Fold in the egg white mixture.

Spoon the filling into the baked pie crusts. Top each tartlet with a few raspberries, and serve.

. . .

*If you liked this recipe,
you will love these as well.*

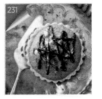

FRANGIPANE TARTLETS
WITH CHOCOLATE
PRALINE TOPPING

CHOCOLATE RASPBERRY
TART

CHOCOLATE MERINGUE
PIE

Serves: 6
Preparation: 30 minutes
    + 40 minutes to chill
    & cool
Cooking: 30 minutes
Level: 2

FRANGIPANE TARTLETS
with chocolate praline topping

Praline
3/4 cup (150 g) superfine (caster) sugar
2 tablespoons water
1/2 cup (50 g) flaked almonds
1 tablespoon each red and green candied (glacé) cherries, diced
1-2 tablespoons chopped mixed candied peel

Crusts
1 cup (150 g) all-purpose (plain) flour
1/3 cup (90 g) unsalted butter
1 tablespoon confectioners' (icing) sugar
3-4 tablespoons iced water

Filling
3 tablespoons unsalted butter, melted
1 large egg
1/4 cup (50 g) superfine (caster) sugar
1 1/2 tablespoons all-purpose (plain) flour
1/2 cup (50 g) finely ground almonds
2 ounces (60 g) dark chocolate, chopped

Praline: Place a large piece of aluminum foil on a baking sheet and lightly grease. Combine the sugar and water in a saucepan over low heat and stir with a wooden spoon until the sugar dissolves. Increase the heat to medium and cook, without stirring, until the mixture turns an amber color, about 10 minutes.

Stir in the almonds, cherries, and candied peel, and pour the mixture evenly onto the prepared baking sheet. Let the praline cool and set, then break into shards.

Crusts: Grease six 3-inch (7-cm) loose-bottomed tartlet pans.

Combine the flour, butter, and confectioners' sugar in a food processor and pulse until the mixture resembles fine bread crumbs. Add enough of the iced water to bring the dough together in a smooth ball. Wrap in plastic wrap (cling film) and chill for 15 minutes.

Roll out the pastry on a lightly floured work surface board until 1/4 inch (5 mm) thick. Cut out six 5-inch (12-cm) rounds and use to line the tartlet pans. Chill for 15 minutes.

Preheat the oven to 375°F (190°C/gas 5). Line the tarts with parchment paper and fill with pastry weights or uncooked rice. Bake for 10 minutes.

Filling: Beat the butter, egg, and sugar in a bowl with an electric mixer until pale and thick. Fold in the flour and almonds.

Remove the paper and weights from the tart shells and spoon in the filling. Bake for 10 minutes, until the filling is firm. Let cool on a wire rack for 10 minutes.

Melt the chocolate in a double boiler over barely simmering water, or in the microwave. Decorate the tartlets with the praline, drizzle with the chocolate, and serve warm or at room temperature.

Serves: 8

Preparation: 45 minutes + 3½–4½ hours to chill

Cooking: 25 minutes

Level: 2

CHOCOLATE RASPBERRY TART

Sweet Tart Pastry

- 2 cups (300 g) all-purpose (plain) flour
- 7 tablespoons (105 g) unsalted butter, cut into small pieces and softened
- 1 cup (150 g) confectioners' (icing) sugar
- ¼ teaspoon salt
- 2 large eggs, lightly beaten

Filling

- 1 cup (150 g) halved raspberries, + 24 whole raspberries
- 10 fresh mint leaves, thinly sliced
- 1 cup (250 ml) heavy (double) cream
- 8 ounces (250 g) dark chocolate, finely chopped
- 2 tablespoons light corn (golden) syrup
- 4 tablespoons (60 g) unsalted butter, cut into small pieces

Sweet Tart Pastry: Put the flour in a bowl and make a well in the center. Add the butter, confectioners' sugar, and salt to the well and mix using your fingertips until a slightly grainy dough forms.

Make another well in the center of the flour mixture and add the eggs. Using your fingers, slowly incorporate the flour mixture into the eggs until the dough begins to come together.

Transfer to a clean work surface and knead the dough briefly, until smooth. Roll the dough into a ball, wrap in plastic wrap (cling film), and chill for 1–2 hours.

Preheat the oven to 375°F (190°C/gas 5). Butter an 8-inch (20-cm) tart pan with a removeable bottom.

Roll out the dough on a lightly floured work surface to ⅛ inch (3 mm) thick. Fit the dough into the prepared pan, pressing it into the edges. Trim the top to fit. Gently prick the base with a fork. Cover with plastic wrap and chill until firm, about 30 minutes.

Line the crust with parchment paper, leaving a 1-inch (2.5-cm) overhang. Fill with pie weights or dried beans. Bake for 20 minutes. Reduce the oven temperature to 350°F (180°C/gas 4), remove the pie weights and parchment paper, and bake for 5 minutes more.

Remove the crust from the pan and transfer to a wire rack to cool.

Filling: Toss the halved raspberries and mint leaves in a bowl. Sprinkle evenly over the base of the cooled crust.

Bring the cream to a boil in a heavy-based pan over medium heat. Remove from the heat and add the chocolate and corn syrup. Beat until smooth and creamy. Beat in the butter, one piece at a time.

Pour the filling into the crust and let cool. Chill for at least 2 hours before serving.

Slice the tart using a sharp knife dipped in hot water. Place slices of tart on serving plates and top with the reserved raspberries.

EASY CHOCOLATE TART
with pears

1/3 cup (70 g) superfine (caster) sugar

2 tablespoons unsweetened cocoa powder

3/4 cup (90 g) pecans

2 ounces (60 g) dark chocolate, chopped

1/3 cup (90 g) cold unsalted butter, finely chopped,

1 large egg

1 (8-ounce/250-g) sheet ready-rolled puff pastry

2 firm, ripe pears

2 teaspoons all-purpose (plain) flour

1 teaspoon vanilla bean paste

2 tablespoons confectioners' (icing) sugar

Heavy (double) cream, to serve

Process 1/4 cup (50 g) of the sugar with the cocoa and pecans in a food processor until finely ground. Add the chocolate, 1/4 cup (60 g) of the butter and the egg, and process until the mixture forms a paste.

Preheat the oven to 450°F (230°C/gas 8). Line a baking sheet with parchment paper.

Place the pastry on the baking sheet. Using a 9-inch (23-cm) cake pan as a guide, cut out a 9-inch (23-cm) round. Place an 8-inch (20-cm) cake pan in the center of the round, and, using it as a guide, score an 8-inch (20-cm) round in the pastry to create a border.

Quarter the pears, then core and cut lengthwise into 1-inch (2.5-cm) thick slices.

Place the flour, remaining sugar, and the pears in a bowl. Add the vanilla bean paste, then use your hands to toss to coat.

Spread the chocolate mixture over the pastry within the scored round. Place pieces of pear over the chocolate mixture. Melt the remaining butter and brush over the pears.

Bake for 15 minutes, then reduce the oven temperature to 375°F (190°C/gas 5) and bake, covering loosely with aluminum foil if the pastry is over-browning, for 25 minutes more, until the pastry is golden brown and puffed.

Set the tart aside on a wire rack for 10 minutes to cool.

Dust the pears with the confectioners' sugar, then, using a chef's blowtorch or under a broiler (grill), caramelize the sugar on the pears.

Serve the tart warm or at room temperature with the cream.

Serves: 8–10

Preparation: 30 minutes
+ 2½ hours to chill
& cool

Cooking: 3–5 minutes

Level: 2

CHOCOLATE MERINGUE PIE

Base

8 ounces (250 g) plain chocolate cookies

½ cup (120 g) unsalted butter, melted

Filling

7 ounces (200 g) milk chocolate, chopped

⅓ cup (90 ml) heavy (double) cream

1 cup (250 g) chocolate hazelnut spread (Nutella), softened

Topping

5 large egg whites

1¼ cups (250 g) superfine (caster) sugar

Base: Lightly grease a 9-inch (23-cm) fluted pie pan with a removeable bottom.

Process the cookies in a food processor until finely chopped. Add the butter and process to combine.

Press the mixture into the base and up the sides of the prepared pan. Place on a baking sheet. Chill for 15 minutes.

Filling: Melt the chocolate and cream in a double boiler over barely simmering water, stirring until melted and smooth. Set aside to cool for 10 minutes.

Spread the cookie crust with the chocolate hazelnut spread. Pour the chocolate mixture over the top. Cover and chill for 2 hours, until firm.

Topping: Preheat the overhead broiler (grill) on high. Beat the egg whites and sugar on medium speed until stiff and glossy.

Spoon the meringue over the chocolate pie. Broil until the meringue is just touched with gold. Let cool for 15 minutes before serving.

. . .

If you liked this recipe,
you will love these as well.

CHOCOLATE TARTLETS
WITH RASPBERRIES

CHOCOLATE RASPBERRY
TART

FROZEN MISSISSIPPI
MUD PIE

Serves: 6–8

Preparation 30 minutes
  + 1½ hours to chill
  & cool

Cooking: 55–60 minutes

Level: 2

PEAR & FRANGIPANE TART
with chocolate sauce

Pastry
1²/₃	cups (250 g) all-purpose (plain) flour
¹/₃	cup (90 g) chilled unsalted butter, cubed
¹/₄	cup (50 g) superfine (caster) sugar
¹/₂	teaspoon salt
2	large egg yolks
2	tablespoons cold water

Pear & Almond Filling
¹/₂	cup (120 g) unsalted butter, softened
³/₄	cup (150 g) superfine (caster) sugar
1	cup (100 g) finely ground almonds
2	large eggs, lightly beaten
1	tablespoon freshly squeezed lemon juice
3	ripe pears, peeled, cored, thickly sliced
2	tablespoons flaked almonds

Chocolate Sauce
6	ounces (180 g) dark chocolate, finely chopped
³/₄	cup (180 ml) heavy (double) cream

Pastry: Combine the flour, butter, sugar, and salt in a food processor and process until the mixture resembles fine bread crumbs. Add the egg yolks and water, and process until the dough just comes together. Turn the dough onto a lightly floured work surface and knead until just smooth. Shape into a disk, cover with plastic wrap (cling film), and chill for 30 minutes.

Roll out the pastry on a lightly floured work surface to ¹/₈ inch (3 mm) thick. Line a 12-inch (30-cm) fluted tart pan with a removable bottom with the pastry. Use a small sharp knife to trim away any excess. Prick the pastry all over with a fork. Chill for 30 minutes.

Preheat the oven to 400°F (200°C/gas 6). Line the pastry case with parchment paper and fill with pastry weights, uncooked rice, or dried beans. Place on a baking sheet and bake for 15 minutes.

Remove the paper and pastry weights and bake for 10–12 minutes more, until golden brown and crisp. Remove from the oven. Reduce the oven temperature to 375°F (190°C/gas 5).

Pear & Almond Filling: Beat the butter, sugar, and almonds in a bowl with an electric mixer on medium speed until pale and creamy. Add the eggs and lemon juice and beat until just combined.

Arrange the pear slices over the base of the pastry crust. Spoon the almond filling over the pears, smoothing the surface with the back of the spoon. Sprinkle with the flaked almonds.

Bake for 30 minutes, until the tart is golden brown and firm to the touch. Remove from the oven. Set aside on a wire rack for 30 minutes to cool.

Chocolate Sauce: Combine the chocolate and cream in a double boiler over barely simmering water, stirring until melted and smooth. Remove from the heat and set aside to cool. Chill for 30 minutes.

Cut the tart into wedges and place on serving plates. Spoon the chocolate cream over the top, and serve.

dessert cakes

This chapter features chilled desserts, from tiramisù, charlottes, and trifles, to cheesecakes, zuccottos, and mousse cakes. They all contain cake and they are all chilled for several hours before serving.

Serves: 8–10

Preparation: 30 minutes
    + 12 hours to chill

Cooking: 5 minutes

Level: 1

. . . . .

Tiramisù is a classic Italian dessert that has become popular the world over in recent years. There are an infinite number of variations; this is our white chocolate and raspberry favorite,

WHITE CHOCOLATE & RASPBERRY TIRAMISÙ

6	ounces (180 g) white chocolate, chopped
¼	cup (30 g) unsweetened cocoa powder
2	cups (500 ml) boiling water
8	ounces (250 g) mascarpone, softened
1¼	cups (300 ml) heavy (double) cream
3	large eggs
⅔	cup (100 g) confectioners' (icing) sugar
	About 20 ladyfingers (sponge fingers)
1	pound (500 g) raspberries
1	cup (300 g) raspberry preserves (jam)

Melt the white chocolate in a double boiler over barely simmering water, or in the microwave. Set aside to cool.

Put the cocoa in a shallow heatproof bowl. Gradually whisk in the boiling water to combine. Set aside to cool for 10 minutes.

Beat the mascarpone in a bowl with an electric mixer on medium speed until smooth. Add the cream and beat until thickened and well combined. Gradually beat in the cooled chocolate.

Beat the eggs and confectioners' sugar in a large bowl until thick and creamy. Fold into the mascarpone mixture.

Dip half the ladyfingers one at a time into the cocoa mixture to coat. Arrange in the base of an 8-cup (2-liter) trifle or pudding dish. Spoon half the mascarpone mixture over the ladyfingers. Top with half the raspberries. Dip the remaining ladyfingers in the cocoa mixture. Arrange over the raspberries, pushing slightly into the mixture. Spoon the remaining mascarpone mixture over the top. Cover and chill overnight.

Heat the raspberry preserves over low heat. Strain through a fine-mesh sieve. Put the remaining raspberries on the tiramisù, drizzle with the raspberry preserves, and serve.

. . .

If you liked this recipe, you will love these as well.

CHOCOLATE RASPBERRY ROLL

CHOCOLATE ESPRESSO TIRAMISU

WHITE CHOCOLATE TRIFLE

Serves: 6
Preparation: 45 minutes
    + 7 hours to freeze
Cooking: 20–25 minutes
Level: 3

. . . . .

Baked Alaska is a classic American dessert named at Delmonico's Restaurant in New York in 1876 in honor of the recently acquired northern-most state. Be sure to bake these baby Alaskas in a very hot oven so that the meringue cooks instantly, insulating the ice cream from the heat.

BABY CHOCOLATE BAKED ALASKAS

Cakes

2	cups (400 g) sugar
1⅓	cups (200 g) all-purpose (plain) flour
1	cup (150 g) unsweetened cocoa powder
2	teaspoons baking powder
2	teaspoons baking soda (bicarbonate of soda)
½	teaspoon salt
1	cup (250 ml) vegetable oil
2	teaspoons vanilla extract (essence)
6	large eggs, separated

Filling

6	cups (1.5 kg) chocolate ice cream

Meringue

12	large egg whites
3	cups (600 g) sugar
	Pinch of cream of tartar

Cakes: Preheat the oven to 350°F (180°C/gas 4). Line two 12 x 17-inch (30 x 43-cm) baking sheets with raised rims with parchment paper.

Mix 1⅓ cups (270 g) of sugar, the flour, cocoa, baking powder, baking soda, and salt in a large bowl. Combine the oil and vanilla in another bowl.

Whisk the egg yolks with an electric mixer on medium speed until pale and thick. Slowly beat the oil mixture into the egg yolks, then add the sugar mixture.

Beat the egg whites, gradually adding the remaining sugar, until stiff peaks form. Fold the egg white mixture into the batter. Divide the batter between the prepared baking sheets.

Bake for 18–20 minutes, until springy to the touch. Let cool.

Filling: Grease six 1¼-cup (300-ml) ramekins. Line with plastic wrap (cling film), leaving an overhang. Cut out six cake circles and use them to line the bottoms of the ramekins. Top each one with ⅓ cup of ice cream. Cut out six more cake circles and place over the ice cream. Freeze until set, about 1 hour. Top each cake with ⅓ cup ice cream, smoothing the surface. Cut out six more cake circles to fit and place over the ice cream. The ramekins should now be full. Cover the cakes with the overhanging plastic wrap and freeze for 6 hours.

To remove from the ramekins, open the plastic wrap, flip the cakes onto a baking sheet, and remove the plastic wrap. Freeze the cakes while you prepare the meringue.

Meringue: Preheat the oven to 500°F (260°C/gas 10). Heat the egg whites, sugar, and cream of tartar in the heatproof bowl of an electric mixer set over a pan of simmering water, whisking often, until the sugar dissolves and the mixture is warm, about 2 minutes. Transfer the bowl to the mixer, and beat until stiff peaks form, about 10 minutes.

Cover each prepared cake with 1 cup of the meringue, making sure the cake is entirely covered. Bake until the meringue is browned, 2–3 minutes. Serve immediately.

CHOCOLATE RASPBERRY ROLL

3	large eggs
3/4	cup (150 g) sugar
1	cup (150 g) self-rising flour
2	tablespoons salted butter, melted
4	cups (1 liter) chocolate ice cream, softened
2	cups (300 g) raspberries
5	ounces (150 g) dark chocolate, chopped
1/3	cup (90 ml) heavy (double) cream
	Grated white chocolate, to serve

Preheat the oven to 375°F (190°C/gas 5). Line a 10 x 12-inch (25 x 30-cm) jelly-roll pan with parchment paper.

Beat the egg whites in a bowl on medium speed until soft peaks form. Gradually add 1/2 cup (100 g) of sugar. Add the egg yolks one at a time, beating well after each addition. Sift the flour three times. Add the butter and flour to the egg mixture. Fold in gently.

Spoon the batter into the prepared pan. Bake for 7–8 minutes, until firm.

Place a large sheet of parchment paper on a work surface. Sprinkle with the remaining sugar. Turn the cake onto the paper. Peel off the lining paper. Roll up the cake from one short side. Let cool.

Stir the raspberries into the softened ice cream. Unroll the cake. Spread with the ice cream mixture. Roll the cake up. Wrap in plastic wrap (cling film). Freeze overnight. Melt the chocolate and cream. Pour over the cake. Sprinkle with the white chocolate. Slice and serve.

Serves: 6–8 Preparation: 30 minutes + 12 hours to freeze Cooking: 7–8 minutes Level: 2

SWEDISH RYE CAKE

12	ounces (350 g) dark chocolate
1/2	cup (120 g) unsalted butter, softened
3/4	cup (120 g) confectioners' (icing) sugar
2	tablespoons unsweetened cocoa
1	tablespoon instant coffee powder
1/4	cup (30 g) finely chopped almonds
1/3	cup (60 g) dried sour cherries
8	ounces (250 g) rye crispbread
1/4	cup (30 g) pistachios, chopped

Line a 12-inch (30-cm) loaf pan with plastic wrap (cling film), leaving an overhang along the long sides of the pan.

Melt the chocolate in a double boiler over barely simmering water, or in the microwave. Set aside to cool a little.

Beat the butter and confectioners' sugar in a large bowl with an electric mixer on medium speed until pale and creamy. Beat in the cocoa and coffee powder. Stir in the chocolate, almonds, and chopped cherries by hand, mixing well.

Line the base of the pan with a layer of crispbread and cover with one-third of the chocolate mixture. Repeat. Mix most of the pistachios into the remaining chocolate mixture and spread over the crispbread in the pan. Cover with another layer of crispbread.
Chill in the refrigerator for 3–4 hours, until set. Turn out onto a plate, sprinkle with the remaining pistachios. Slice and serve.

Serves: 6–8 Preparation: 30 minutes + 3–4 hours to chill Level: 1

You can vary this ice cream cake in endless ways: try it with vanilla ice cream with 1 cup of chocolate chips stirred into it, instead of the raspberries, or replace the raspberries with sliced strawberries or fresh blueberries.

This unusual dessert cake is surprisingly good.

Serves: 6-8
Preparation: 30 minutes
  + 4-12 hours to chill
Level: 2

· · · · ·

This tiramisù uses cantuccini, the traditional almond biscotti from the Tuscan town of Prato. They are now widely available in supermarkets everywhere, but if you can't find them, use any crisp biscotti in their place. You could also use our own Chocolate pistachio biscotti (see page 59).

CHOCOLATE ESPRESSO TIRAMISÙ

3½ ounces (100 g) dark chocolate

2¼ cups (300 ml) brewed espresso

1 tablespoon vanilla sugar

6 tablespoons (90 ml) Cointreau

2 unwaxed oranges

8 ounces (250 g) chocolate cantuccini (biscotti)

1 pound (500 g) mascarpone

2 tablespoons superfine (caster) sugar

2 teaspoons vanilla bean paste, or 2 vanilla pods

2 tablespoons unsweetened cocoa powder

Prepare the dessert in a deep glass bowl about 8 inches (20 cm) in diameter.

To make chocolate shavings, chill the chocolate first and shave it off the bar with a vegetable peeler or knife. Set aside.

Sweeten the espresso with the vanilla sugar and 2 tablespoons of the Cointreau. Finely grate the zest of the oranges (keeping it for decoration later), then squeeze them and strain the juice.

Put the cantuccini into a shallow dish and pour in the espresso and 2 tablespoons of the orange juice so they are completely covered.

Beat the mascarpone with the sugar, remaining Cointreau, and the vanilla bean paste in a bowl with an electric mixer at medium speed. If you are using vanilla pods, split them open lengthwise and scrape the seeds into the mascarpone. Drizzle enough orange juice into the mixture to loosen it. Continue whisking until it is light and airy and looks glossy. Pour any remaining juice into the dish with the cantuccini.

Use about half of the cantuccini to line the bottom of the glass bowl. Spoon half the mascarpone mixture on top, sprinkle with a tablespoon of cocoa and a layer of chocolate shavings. Place the remaining biscotti on top, followed by the remaining mascarpone, the remaining cocoa, and the chocolate shavings.

Decorate with orange zest and refrigerate for at least 4 hours before serving.

· · ·

If you liked this recipe, you will love these as well.

WHITE CHOCOLATE
& RASPBERRY TIRAMISÙ

WHITE CHOCOLATE
TRIFLE

BOOZY CHOCOLATE
BERRY CAKE

Serves: 6–8

Preparation: 30 minutes
    + 4–12 hours to chill

Level: 1

· · · · ·

Trifle is a traditional English dessert made with sponge cake, custard, and whipped cream. The first trifle recipe appeared in *The Good Housewife's Jewel*, one of the earliest English cook books, first published in 1596.

WHITE CHOCOLATE TRIFLE

Trifle

1   pound (500 g) storebought Madeira or foam (sponge) cake

5   tablespoons apricot preserves (jam)

4   tablespoons sherry

2   tablespoons freshly squeezed orange juice

2   (18-ounce/560-g) cans apricots, drained

2   (14-ounce/400-g) cans peaches, drained

8   ounces (250 g) white chocolate

1   cup (250 g) mascarpone

1   cup (250 ml) vanilla custard (see page 285), or use storebought fresh custard

1   teaspoon vanilla extract (essence)

1   teaspoon freshly grated unwaxed orange zest

1¼ cups (300 ml) heavy (double) cream

Decoration

2   tablespoons pistachios, chopped

    White chocolate curls

Trifle: Cut the cake into thin slices. Sandwich the slices together with the apricot preserves. Use the cake to line the base of a large glass bowl or eight 1-cup (250-ml) glasses. Drizzle with 3 tablespoons of the sherry and the orange juice. Slice half the apricots and arrange on top.

Put the peaches and remaining apricots into a food processor and blend to a purée. Pour over the apricots and leave to soak up the alcohol and juices.

Melt the white chocolate in a double boiler over barely simmering water, or in the microwave. Set aside to cool a little.

Beat the mascarpone and custard with an electric mixer on low speed in a large bowl. Add the vanilla, orange zest, and remaining 1 tablespoon of sherry. Gently beat in the chocolate.

In a separate bowl, whip the cream until soft peaks form. Fold half the whipped cream into the chocolate mixture. Spoon over the fruit in an even layer, and spread or pipe the remaining cream on top.

Chill for 4–12 hours before serving.

Decoration: Sprinkle with the pistachios and chocolate curls and serve.

· · ·

If you liked this recipe, you will love these as well.

WHITE CHOCOLATE & RASPBERRY TIRAMISÙ

BOOZY CHOCOLATE BERRY CAKE

MOZART BOMBE

Serves: 8–12

Preparation: 30 minutes
    + 7 hours to chill

Cooking: 1 hour

Level: 2

BOOZY CHOCOLATE BERRY CAKE

Cake

1⅓	cups (330 ml) espresso coffee
7	ounces (200 g) dark chocolate, grated
⅔	cup (150 ml) Marsala wine
1	cup (250 g) butter, chopped
2	cups (400 g) firmly packed brown sugar
2	cups (300 g) all-purpose (plain) flour
1	teaspoon baking powder
2	large eggs, beaten

Mascarpone Cream

1	cup (250 ml) heavy (double) cream
8	ounces (250 g) mascarpone
⅓	cup (50 g) confectioners' (icing) sugar
¼	cup (60 ml) Marsala

Boozy Berries

2	cups (300 g) raspberries
2	cups (300 g) blueberries
1	tablespoon confectioners' (icing) sugar
¼	cup (60 ml) orange-flavored liqueur

Cake: Preheat the oven to 300°F (150°C/gas 2). Line the base and sides of two 5 x 9-inch (13 x 23-cm) loaf pans with parchment paper.

Combine the coffee, chocolate, Marsala, and butter in a medium saucepan over low heat. Stir until melted and smooth. Set aside for 5 minutes to cool. Add the brown sugar and stir to combine.

Sift the flour and baking powder over the chocolate mixture and stir to combine. Stir in the eggs. Spoon into the prepared pans.

Bake for 1 hour, until a toothpick inserted into the center comes out clean. Let cool completely.

Mascarpone Cream: Beat the cream until soft peaks form.

Combine the mascarpone, confectioners' sugar, and Marsala in a medium bowl. Fold in the cream. Use a large serrated knife to cut each cake into three even layers.

Clean one of the loaf pans and line with plastic wrap (cling film), allowing the sides to overhang.

Place a layer of cake in the base. Spread with one-fifth of the mascarpone mixture. Continue layering with cake and mascarpone mixture, finishing with a layer of cake. Cover with plastic wrap and chill in the refrigerator for 6 hours.

Boozy Berries: Combine the raspberries, blueberries, confectioners' sugar, and orange liqueur in a bowl. Set aside for 1 hour to macerate.

Carefully remove the cake from the pan using the overhanging plastic. Place on a serving platter. Slice and serve, spooning some of the boozy berries over each portion.

Serves: 8–12
Preparation: 30 minutes
+ 12 hours to chill
Cooking: 25–35 minutes
Level: 2

CHILLED CHOCOLATE ORANGE TORTE

Torte

½	cup (120 g) unsalted butter
12	ounces (350 g) dark chocolate
5	ounces (150 g) dark orange chocolate
1	tablespoon orange liqueur (Cointreau, Grand Marnier)
6	large eggs, separated
½	cup (100 g) firmly packed light brown (golden caster) sugar
½	cup (120 ml) heavy (double) cream, lightly whipped

Frosting

½	cup (120 ml) heavy (double) cream
4	ounces (120 g) dark chocolate, coarsely chopped
1	tablespoon orange liqueur (Cointreau, Grand Marnier)
	Fresh blueberries, to serve
	Fresh cream, to serve

Torte: Preheat the oven to 350°F (180°C/gas 4). Grease an 8-inch (20-cm) springform pan. Line the base with parchment paper.

Melt the butter and both types of chocolate in a double boiler over barely simmering water, stirring until smooth. Remove from the heat, stir in the orange liqueur, and set aside to cool a little.

Beat the egg yolks and sugar in a bowl with an electric mixer on high speed until pale and thick. With the mixer on low speed, gradually beat in the melted chocolate. Fold in the cream by hand.

Beat the egg whites in a separate bowl with the mixer on medium speed until stiff peaks form. Fold a large spoonful of the egg whites into the chocolate mixture. Then fold in the remaining egg whites until well incorporated.

Spoon the batter into the prepared pan. Bake for 25–35 minutes, until risen but still a little wobbly in the center.

Let cool in the pan for 10 minutes. Run a knife around the edges, unclip and remove the pan sides, and let cool completely. Cover and chill overnight.

Frosting: Melt the cream with the chocolate and Cointreau in a double boiler over barely simmering water, stirring until smooth. Continue stirring until cool and beginning to thicken.

Place the torte on a wire rack and spread with the frosting. When completely set, cut the torte into small slices and serve with the blueberries and cream.

. . .

If you liked this recipe, you will love these as well.

BOOZY CHOCOLATE
BERRY CAKE

CHILLED MUD CAKE
WITH COFFEE CREAM

CHOCOLATE ALMOND
TORTE

Serves: 12
Preparation: 30 minutes
    + 1¼ hours to chill
Cooking: 12–13 minutes
Level: 2

. . . . .

When using leaves or flowers in baking always make sure you buy only the ones that are certified as edible. They should not be toxic, nor should they have been sprayed or treated with any chemicals.

CHILLED MUD CAKE
with coffee cream

Cake
1	pound (500 g) dark chocolate
2	tablespoons light corn (golden) syrup
½	cup (120 g) unsalted butter
4	large eggs
1	tablespoon superfine (caster) sugar
1	tablespoon all-purpose (plain) flour

Coffee Cream
2	tablespoons instant coffee
1	tablespoon boiling water
8	ounces (250 g) mascarpone
⅓	cup (50 g) confectioners' (icing) sugar

Chocolate Leaves
5	ounces (150 g) dark chocolate, chopped
24	untreated, non-toxic leaves, such as lemon or rose leaves

Cake: Preheat the oven to 450°F (230°C/gas 8). Grease an 8-inch (20-cm) springform pan. Line the base with parchment paper.

Melt the chocolate, corn syrup, and butter in a double boiler over barely simmering water. Set aside to cool slightly.

Beat the eggs and sugar in a large bowl with an electric mixer on medium speed until very thick and pale. Gently fold in the flour, followed by the chocolate mixture, until just combined.

Spoon the batter into the prepared pan. Bake for 12–13 minutes, until risen and just firm to the touch.

Run a knife around the edges of the pan. Let cool on a wire rack for 15 minutes, then chill in the refrigerator for 1 hour.

Coffee Cream: Dissolve the coffee in the water and set aside to cool.

Beat the mascarpone, coffee mixture, and confectioners' sugar in a bowl until well mixed. Chill until ready to use.

Chocolate Leaves: Melt the chocolate in a double boiler over barely simmering water. Set aside to cool slightly.

Brush one side of each leaf with the melted chocolate. Place on a large platter or baking sheet to set. When cool, peel the leaves off.

Slice the cake and serve with a dollop of coffee cream, and a chocolate leaf or two on top.

. . .

If you liked this recipe, you will love these as well.

MINI CHOCOLATE
MUD CAKES

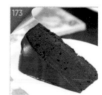

CHOCOLATE MUD CAKE

CHILLED CHOCOLATE
ORANGE TORTE

. . . . .

If the cake has been in the freezer overnight, bring it out and let sit at room temperature for 15–20 minutes before serving.

COOL CHOCOLATE PIE

Crust

2   cups (250 g) finely crushed plain chocolate cookies

¹⁄₄ cup (60 g) unsalted butter, melted

2   ounces (60 g) dark chocolate, chopped

2   tablespoons unsweetened cocoa powder

Filling

1   teaspoon instant espresso coffee

¹⁄₃ cup (90 ml) boiling water

5   ounces (150 g) dark chocolate, chopped + extra, finely grated, to finish

3   large eggs, separated + 1 large yolk

1   teaspoon vanilla extract (essence)

¹⁄₃ cup (90 ml) almond liqueur (Amaretto)

¹⁄₄ cup (50 g) superfine (caster) sugar

Crust: Grease an 8-inch (20-cm) springform pan and line with plastic wrap (cling film).

Mix the cookie crumbs with the melted butter, chocolate, and cocoa. Press the mixture into the base of the prepared pan. Chill in the refrigerator while you prepare the filling.

Filling: Dissolve the coffee in the boiling water. Place the coffee and chocolate in a double boiler over barely simmering water and stir until smooth. Remove from the heat and let cool completely.

Add the egg yolks, vanilla, and almond liqueur to the cooled chocolate mixture, stirring well to combine.

Beat the egg whites in a separate bowl with an electric mixer on medium speed until soft peaks form. Gradually beat in the sugar until stiff and glossy.

Gently fold the egg white mixture into the chocolate mixture. Pour over the chilled base and freeze for at least 4 hours, or overnight.

Sprinkle with the finely grated chocolate just before serving.

. . .

If you liked this recipe, you will love these as well.

CHOCOLATE CHESTNUT
MOUSSE CAKE

DOUBLE CHOCOLATE
MOUSSE CAKE

MILK CHOCOLATE
CHEESECAKE

CHOCOLATE CHESTNUT MOUSSE CAKE

Crust

3	large eggs
1/2	cup (100 g) superfine (caster) sugar
1/3	cup (50 g) all-purpose (plain) flour
1/3	cup (50 g) unsweetened cocoa powder
1/2	cup (120 g) salted butter, melted
2	tablespoons brandy

Chestnut Mousse

1	(14-ounce/400-g) can unsweetened chestnut purée
2	large eggs, separated
14	ounces (400 g) dark chocolate, grated
2 1/2	cups (600 ml) heavy (double) cream
	Unsweetened cocoa powder, to dust
	Fresh cherries, to decorate

Crust: Preheat the oven to 400°F (200°C/gas 6). Grease a 10-inch (25-cm) springform pan, then line the base with parchment paper.

Beat the eggs and sugar in a large bowl with an electric mixer on medium speed until pale and thick. Sift the flour and cocoa over the mixture, then gently fold them in. Drizzle with the butter, folding it in as well. Spoon the batter into the prepared pan.

Bake for 8–10 minutes, until risen and firm to the touch. Let cool in the pan on a wire rack.

Chestnut Mousse: Beat the chestnut purée and egg yolks in a bowl with an electric mixer on low speed until smooth.

Melt the chocolate and half the cream in a double boiler over barely simmering water until smooth. Remove from the heat, let cool a little, then stir into the chestnut mixture.

Beat the egg whites in a separate bowl until stiff. Beat the remaining cream until thick. Fold the cream into the chocolate mixture, then carefully fold in the egg whites.

Drizzle the brandy over the base, then pour the chestnut mousse over the top. Level the surface and chill overnight until firm.

To serve, carefully remove from the pan, strip off the paper and slide onto a serving plate. Dust generously with the cocoa and top with the cherries just before serving.

. . .

If you liked this recipe, you will love these as well.

259

268 281

COOL CHOCOLATE PIE

DOUBLE CHOCOLATE MOUSSE CAKE

RUSSIAN SNOWFLAKES

. . . . .

Serve the Mozart bombe chilled, ideally accompanied by one of the composer's beautiful concertos.

MOZART BOMBE

Cake

6	large eggs, separated
3/4	cup (150 g) sugar
1	tablespoon vanilla sugar, or 1 teaspoon vanilla extract
	Finely grated zest of 1 unwaxed lemon
1	cup (150 g) all-purpose flour

Filling

1	(15-ounce/450-g) jar (sour) cherries, in syrup
3	tablespoons orange liqueur
1	tablespoon brandy
2	cups (500 ml) heavy (double) cream
3	tablespoons sugar

Glaze

6	ounces (180 g) bittersweet chocolate
3/4	cup (180 ml) heavy whipping cream
3	tablespoons pistachio nuts, finely chopped
	Reserved cherries, for decoration

Cake: Butter the bottom half of an 8-inch (20-cm) domed cake pan and dust with flour. Preheat the oven to 350°F (180°C/gas 4).

Beat the egg yolks in a bowl with ½ cup (100 g) of sugar and the vanilla with an electric mixer on high speed until thick and pale. Stir in the lemon zest.

Beat the egg whites with the mixer until they stand in soft peaks. Gradually beat in the remaining ¼ cup (50 g) of sugar until smooth and glossy. Fold one-third of the egg whites into the yolk mixture. Fold in the remaining egg whites.

Sift the flour over the batter and fold in gently. Spoon the batter into the prepared pan.

Bake for 25–35 minutes, until golden and springy to the touch. Invert onto a wire rack and turn once while cooling to stop it sticking.

Filling: Drain the cherries, reserving the syrup. Pour ¾ cup (180 ml) of the syrup into a small bowl and mix with the orange liqueur and brandy.

Use a long serrated knife to cut the cooled cake horizontally into 8–10 circles. Place the circles separately on a work surface and brush generously with the syrup.

Coarsely chop the cherries. Beat the cream and sugar in a bowl with an electric mixer until stiff. Stir in the cherries by hand.

Build the bombe, beginning with the largest circle of cake. Lift it with a spatula onto a serving plate and spread evenly with the cherry cream. Top with the next biggest circle, and spread with filling. Repeat the layers until you reach the top. Finish with the smallest circle cut-side down. Chill while you make the glaze, so the layers don't slide apart.

Glaze: Break the chocolate into a heatproof bowl. Bring the cream to a boil and pour over the chocolate. Stir until melted. Whisk until cool.

Pour the glaze over the bombe, smoothing the sides. Sprinkle with pistachios and decorate with cherries. Chill for 3–4 hours, until set.

Serves: 6–8
Preparation: 30 minutes
    + 5–12 hours to chill
Cooking: 35 minutes
Level: 3

· · · · ·

A Zuccotto is a classic dessert from the Italian city of Florence. Its shape is said to be inspired by the city's famous Cathedral dome, while its name is thought to derive from the name of a cardinal's skullcap (*zucchetto*, in Italian).

CLASSIC ZUCCOTTO

Cake

4	large eggs
³⁄₄	cup (150 g) sugar
²⁄₃	cup (100 g) all-purpose (plain) flour
2	tablespoons cornstarch (cornflour)
¹⁄₄	cup (60 g) salted butter, melted

Filling

1	cup (200 g) sugar
1	cup (250 ml) water
3	tablespoons brandy
3	tablespoons rum
2	cups (500 ml) heavy (double) cream
¹⁄₃	cup (50 g) confectioners' (icing) sugar
¹⁄₃	cup (30 g) finely ground almonds
¹⁄₃	cup (30 g) finely ground hazelnuts
¹⁄₄	cup (40 g) mixed candied peel, chopped
6	ounces (180 g) dark chocolate, grated

Cake: Preheat the oven to 350°F (180°C/gas 4). Grease a 9-inch (23-cm) springform pan. Line the base and sides with parchment paper.

Beat the eggs and sugar in a bowl with an electric mixer on medium speed until pale and thick. Sift in the flour and cornstarch and gently fold until just combined. Add the butter and fold until combined. Spoon the batter into the prepared pan.

Bake for 30 minutes, until the cake springs back when lightly tapped. Turn out onto a wire rack and let cool completely.

Filling: Stir the sugar and water in a saucepan over medium heat until the sugar has dissolved and the mixture comes to a boil. Simmer for 5 minutes. Remove from the heat. Add the brandy and rum and let cool.

Use a large serrated knife to cut the cake into three layers. Reserve one layer of cake. Cut the remaining layers into triangles.

Moisten the edges of a domed 2-quart (2-liter) mold or metal bowl with a little of the syrup and line with the cake triangles. Brush with the remaining syrup.

Beat the cream until thick. Gently fold the confectioners' sugar, almonds, hazelnuts, candied fruit, and 5 ounces (150 g) of chocolate into the cream. Spoon the cream mixture into the mold. Top with the reserved cake layer.

Refrigerate for 5 hours, or overnight.

Dip the mold briefly into hot water. Invert onto a serving plate. Sprinkle with the remaining grated chocolate. Slice and serve.

· · · ·

If you liked this recipe, you will love these as well.

CHOCOLATE RASPBERRY ROLL

MOZART BOMBE

CHOCOLATE CHERRY ZUCCOTTO

Serves: 6–8
Preparation: 30 minutes
    + 6–12 hours to chill
Cooking: 30 minutes
Level: 3

. . . . .

If you are pushed for time, you could make the zuccotto on this page (and also the one on page 331), using a 9-inch (23-cm) storebought foam (sponge) cake.

CHOCOLATE CHERRY ZUCCOTTO

Cake

4	large eggs
3/4	cup (150 g) sugar
1/2	cup (75 g) all-purpose (plain) flour
2	tablespoons cornstarch (cornflour)
2	tablespoons unsweetened cocoa powder
1/4	cup (60 g) salted butter, melted

Filling

6	tablespoons (90 ml) Marsala
3 1/2	ounces (100 g) dark chocolate, coarsely chopped
10	ounces (300 g) fresh ricotta cheese
8	ounces (250 g) mascarpone
1/2	cup (100 g) superfine (caster) sugar
1/4	cup (30 g) candied (glacé) peel, chopped
1/4	cup (30 g) pistachios, chopped
1/4	cup (30 g) coarsely chopped candied (glacé) cherries
1/4	cup (30 g) toasted slivered almonds
	Unsweetened cocoa powder, to dust

Cake: Preheat the oven to 350°F (180°C/gas 4). Grease a 9-inch (23-cm) springform pan. Line the base and sides with parchment paper.

Beat the eggs and sugar in a bowl with an electric mixer on medium speed until pale and thick. Sift in the flour, cornstarch, and cocoa and gently fold until just combined. Add the butter and fold until combined. Spoon the batter into the prepared pan.

Bake for 30 minutes, until the cake springs back when lightly tapped. Turn out onto a wire rack and let cool completely.

Filling: Line a 6-cup (1.5-liter) pudding basin with plastic wrap (cling film), leaving a generous overhang.

Use a large serrated knife to cut the cake into three layers. Reserve one layer of cake. Cut the remaining layers into triangles.

Line the base and sides of the prepared basin with the cake triangles. Brush with 4 tablespoons of Marsala.

Melt the chocolate in a double boiler over barely simmering water. Combine the ricotta, mascarpone, sugar, and remaining Marsala in a bowl. Add the ricotta mixture to the chocolate, stirring to combine. Stir in the candied peel, pistachios, cherries, and almonds. Spoon into the basin, smoothing the surface. Top with the reserved cake layer.

Cover with plastic wrap and top with a plate. Place a heavy object on top to compress the filling. Chill in the refrigerator for 6–12 hours.

Turn out onto a plate and remove the plastic. Dust with cocoa. Cut into wedges and serve.

. . .

*If you liked this recipe,
you will love these as well.*

CHOCOLATE RASPBERRY
ROLL

MOZART BOMBE

CLASSIC ZUCCOTTO

Serves: 8–10
Preparation: 30 minutes
        + 12 hours to freeze
Cooking: 5 minutes
Level: 2

DOUBLE CHOCOLATE MOUSSE CAKE

15   ounces (450 g) dark
      chocolate, coarsely
      chopped

4   large eggs,
      separated

1¼   cups (250 g)
      superfine (caster)
      sugar

2   cups (500 ml) heavy
      (double) cream

⅓   cup (90 ml) rum

2   cups (500 ml)
      strong black coffee

15   ounces (450 g)
      ladyfingers (sponge
      fingers)

      Unsweetened cocoa
      powder, to dust

Melt the chocolate in a double boiler over barely simmering water, or in the microwave. Set aside to cool.

Beat the egg yolks with half the sugar in a bowl with an electric mixer on medium speed until pale and thick. Beat the cream in a separate bowl until thickened.

Fold the chocolate into the egg mixture, then carefully fold in the cream. Chill in the refrigerator.

Add the remaining sugar and the rum to the hot coffee, stirring to dissolve the sugar.

Dip half the ladyfingers into the coffee mixture and place a layer in a 10-inch (25-cm) springform pan, completely covering the base. Spread the chocolate mixture over top.

Dip the remaining ladyfingers in the coffee mixture and place over the top. Cover and freeze overnight.

Transfer to the refrigerator 30 minutes before serving. Dust with cocoa, slice, and serve.

. . .

If you liked this recipe, you will love these as well.

COOL CHOCOLATE PIE   CHOCOLATE CHESTNUT   RUSSIAN SNOWFLAKES
                            MOUSSE CAKE

Serves: 6–8
Preparation: 30 minutes
    + 4 hours to chill
Cooking: 17–20 minutes
Level: 1

CHOCOLATE ALMOND TORTE

Cake

5   ounces (150 g) dark chocolate, coarsely chopped

$^2/_3$ cup (150 g) unsalted butter

$^1/_2$ cup (100 g) superfine (caster) sugar

5   large eggs, separated

1   teaspoon vanilla extract (essence)

1   cup (100 g) finely ground almonds

     Raspberries, to serve

White Chocolate Sauce

3   ounces (90 g) white chocolate, finely chopped

$^1/_2$ cup (120 ml) heavy (double) cream

$^1/_2$ teaspoon vanilla extract (essence)

Cake: Preheat the oven to 400°F (200°C/gas 6). Grease a 9-inch (23-cm) springform pan and line the base with parchment paper.

Melt the chocolate in a double boiler over barely simmering water, or in the microwave. Set aside to cool slightly.

Beat the butter and sugar in a bowl with an electric mixer on medium-high speed until pale and creamy. Add the egg yolks one at a time, beating until just combined after each addition.

With the mixer on low speed, gradually beat in the melted chocolate, vanilla, and almonds. Beat the egg whites in a separate bowl until stiff peaks form. Fold the egg whites into the batter. Spoon the batter into the prepared pan.

Bake for 10 minutes. Decrease the oven temperature to 325°F (170°C/gas 3) and bake for 7–10 minutes more. The center of the cake should still be jiggly. Let cool completely in the pan.

Cover and chill in the refrigerator for 4 hours.

White Chocolate Sauce: Combine the white chocolate in a heatproof bowl. Heat the cream in a small saucepan until just before it comes to a boil. Pour over the chocolate in the bowl and stir until smooth. Stir in the vanilla.

Remove the cake from the pan and cut into wedges. Spoon some warm sauce over each portion, scatter with some raspberries, and serve.

. . .

*If you liked this recipe,
you will love these as well.*

CHILLED CHOCOLATE
ORANGE TORTE

CHILLED MUD CAKE
WITH COFFEE CREAM

CHOCOLATE CHESTNUT
MOUSSE CAKE

Serves: 6–8
Preparation: 30 minutes
    + time to churn &
    10 hours to freeze
Cooking: 10–12 minutes
Level: 3

FROZEN MISSISSIPPI MUD PIE

Base

1 1/2 cups (185 g) plain chocolate wafer (biscuit) crumbs

3 1/2 ounces (100 g) unsalted butter, melted

2 tablespoons light brown sugar

Filling

8 large egg yolks

1/2 cup (100 g) superfine (caster) sugar

1 3/4 cups (430 ml) heavy (double) cream

1 1/2 cups (375 ml) milk

8 ounces (250 g) dark chocolate, coarsely chopped

Topping

1 cup (250 ml) heavy (double) cream

1 tablespoon confectioners' (icing) sugar

2 ounces (60 g) dark chocolate, grated, to decorate

Base: Preheat the oven to 350°F (180°C/gas 4).

Place the cookie crumbs, butter, and brown sugar in a small bowl and stir to combine. Press into the base and up the sides of a 9-inch (23-cm) pie pan.

Bake for 10–12 minutes, until lightly toasted. Remove from the oven and set aside to cool.

Filling: Beat the egg yolks and sugar in a medium bowl with an electric mixer on medium-high speed until pale and thick.

Place the cream and milk in a large saucepan over medium heat and bring to a boil. Gradually pour half of the cream into the yolk mixture, stirring to combine.

Place the chocolate in a small heatproof bowl and pour in the remaining hot cream, stirring until melted. Add to the egg mixture and stir to combine.

Return the chocolate mixture to the pan and simmer over low heat, stirring constantly, until thickened enough to coat the back of the spoon. Do not allow the mixture to boil. Remove from the heat, transfer to a medium bowl, and refrigerate until cooled.

Pour the cooled chocolate custard into an ice-cream machine and churn according to manufacturer's instructions until almost frozen. Spoon the ice cream into the prepared pan.

Cover with plastic wrap (cling film) and freeze for 2 hours.

Topping: Beat the cream and confectioners' sugar in a medium bowl with an electric mixer until soft peaks form.

Place the cream in a pastry (piping) bag fitted with a star-shaped nozzle. Pipe cream around the border of the pie and decorate with grated chocolate.

Cover and return to the freezer for at least 8 hours. Slice and serve.

Serves: 6–8
Preparation: 20 minutes
  + 2 hours to chill
Cooking: 20–30 minutes
Level: 2

MINI MILK CHOCOLATE CHEESECAKES

Crust

2	cups (250 g) graham crackers or digestive biscuit crumbs
5	tablespoons (75 g) unsalted butter, melted
½	teaspoon ground cinnamon

Filling

8	ounces (250 g) light cream cheese
4	ounces (120 g) fresh ricotta, drained
1	teaspoon vanilla extract (essence)
⅓	cup (70 g) superfine (caster) sugar
2	large eggs
1	tablespoon self-rising flour
5	ounces (150 g) milk chocolate, grated
	Milk chocolate curls, to decorate

Crust: Preheat the oven to 325°F (170°C/gas 3). Grease six to eight small tartlet pans.

Put the cookie crumbs in a bowl and stir in the butter and cinnamon, mixing until well combined. Spoon into the prepared tartlet pans. Press down firmly. Bake for 10–12 minutes.

Filling: Beat the cream cheese, ricotta, vanilla, and sugar in a bowl with an electric mixer on medium speed until smooth. Beat in the eggs and flour. Stir in the chocolate by hand.

Spoon the mixture evenly over the crusts. Bake for 12–15 minutes, until just set. Let cool completely in the pans, then chill for at least 2 hours.

Decorate with the milk chocolate curls and serve.

. . .

If you liked this recipe, you will love these as well.

276

MILK CHOCOLATE
CHEESECAKE

278

WHITE CHOCOLATE
CHEESECAKE WITH
RASPBERRY COULIS

286

MARBLED CHEESECAKE

Serves: 8–12

Preparation: 45 minutes
+ 7 hours to cool
& chill

Cooking: 1 hour

Level: 2

MILK CHOCOLATE CHEESECAKE

Crust

12   ounces (350 g) plain chocolate cookies

1/2   cup (120 g) unsalted butter, melted

Filling

2   cups (350 g) milk chocolate chips

1   pound (500 g) cream cheese, softened

1/2   cup (100 g) sugar

1/4   teaspoon salt

3   large eggs, lightly beaten

1/4   cup (60 ml) milk

2   teaspoons vanilla extract (essence)

Topping

1 1/2 cups (375 ml) sour cream

2   tablespoons sugar

Crust: Preheat the oven to 350°F (180°C/gas 4).

Pulse the chocolate cookies in a food processor until fine crumbs form. Add the butter and pulse several times to combine. Transfer to a 9-inch (23-cm) springform pan. Press the mixture into the bottom and up the sides of the pan.

Bake the crust for 10 minutes, until just crisp. Let cool in the pan on a wire rack while you prepare the filling.

Filling: Melt the chocolate chips in a double boiler over barely simmering water, or in the microwave. Set aside to cool.

Beat the cream cheese, sugar, and salt in a bowl with an electric mixer on medium speed until smooth. With the mixer on low speed, add the eggs, milk, and vanilla, beating until just blended. Add the chocolate and beat until combined. Pour the filling mixture into crust, smoothing the top.

Bake for about 45 minutes, until the cheesecake is almost set, but still slightly jiggly in the center.

Topping: Stir the sour cream and sugar in a bowl until the sugar dissolves. Set aside.

Remove the cheesecake from the oven and spread with the topping. Bake for 5 minutes, until the sour cream is set. Let cool completely in the pan on a wire rack, at least 1 hour.

Cover and refrigerate for at least 6 hours before serving.

. . .

If you liked this recipe,
you will love these as well.

CHOCOLATE
CHEESECAKE BARS

MINI MILK CHOCOLATE
CHEESECAKES

DOUBLE CHOCOLATE
CHEESECAKE

Serves: 8–12

Preparation: 30 minutes
 + 6 hours to cool
 & chill

Cooking: 1 hour 20
 minutes

Level: 2

WHITE CHOCOLATE CHEESECAKE
with raspberry coulis

Crust

1⅓	cups (200 g) graham cracker or digestive biscuit crumbs
⅓	cup (90 g) butter melted
14	ounces (400 g) white chocolate, coarsely chopped + extra, to decorate
1	cup (250 ml) heavy (double) cream
1½	cups (375 ml) cream cheese, softened
4	large eggs
1	teaspoon vanilla extract (essence)

Raspberry Coulis

2	cups (300 g) fresh raspberries
2	tablespoons confectioners' (icing) sugar
2	tablespoons freshly squeezed lemon juice

Crust: Preheat the oven to 350°F (180°C/gas 4). Line the base of a 9-inch (23-cm) springform pan with baking parchment.

Chop the cookie crumbs and butter in a food processor until they resemble bread crumbs. Transfer the mixture to the prepared pan and press down firmly. Bake for 10 minutes. Set aside to cool.

Reduce the oven temperature to 275°F (140°C/gas 1). Wrap a double layer of aluminum foil around the base and sides of the pan to make it waterproof.

Combine the chocolate and cream in a heavy-based saucepan over low heat and stir until melted and smooth. Set aside to cool slightly.

Beat the cream cheese, eggs, and vanilla with the cooled chocolate until smooth.

Put the springform pan in a deep roasting pan. Pour the filling over the crust. Fill the roasting pan with enough boiling water to come halfway up the sides of the springform pan.

Bake for 1 hour, then turn the oven off. Leave to cool in the oven with the door slightly ajar for 2 hours.

Lift the cheesecake from the water, discarding the foil. Cover with plastic wrap (cling film) and chill for at least 4 hours.

Raspberry Coulis: Mash the raspberries in a bowl with the confectioners' sugar and lemon juice. Strain through a fine-mesh sieve to remove the seeds. Sprinkle the cheesecake with extra chocolate. Slice and serve with the raspberry coulis.

. . .

If you liked this recipe, you will love these as well.

WHITE CHOCOLATE & RASPBERRY TIRAMISÙ

MINI MILK CHOCOLATE CHEESECAKES

WHITE LADYFINGER CHEESECAKE WITH EDIBLE FLOWERS

Serves: 8-12
Preparation: 30 minutes
    + 1¼ hours to chill
Cooking: 60–70 minutes
Level: 1

· · · · ·

This Russian recipe is named for the scattering of dough over the filling, which is said to look like snowflakes on the ground.

RUSSIAN SNOWFLAKES

Cake Base

2½ cups (375 g) all-purpose (plain) flour

3 tablespoons unsweetened cocoa powder

3 teaspoons baking powder

1 cup (200 g) sugar

1 teaspoon vanilla extract (essence)

¾ cup (200 g) unsalted butter, softened

1 large egg

Filling

⅓ cup (90 g) unsalted butter

¾ cup (150 g) sugar

1 tablespoon vanilla sugar, or 1 teaspoon vanilla bean paste

3 large eggs

2 cups (500 g) cream cheese or quark

¾ cup (180 ml) heavy (double) cream

1 tablespoon semolina or custard powder

Cake Base: Sift the flour, cocoa, and baking powder into a bowl. Stir in the sugar, vanilla, butter, and egg. Knead into a dough using a dough hook or by hand.

Transfer to a lightly floured work surface and knead until smooth. If the dough is very sticky, chill for 15 minutes.

Preheat the oven to 350°F (180°C/gas 4). Lightly oil a 10-inch (26-cm) springform pan. Line the base and 1 inch (2.5 cm) up the sides of the pan with three-quarters of the cake base. Wrap the remaining dough in plastic wrap (cling film) and chill while you prepare the filling.

Filling: Beat the butter, sugar, and vanilla in a bowl with an electric mixer on medium-high speed until pale and creamy. Add the eggs one at a time, beating until just combined after each addition.

With the mixer on low speed, beat in the cream cheese, cream, and semolina until well combined.

Spoon the filling into the cake base. Finally, pull off little pieces of the reserved dough and scatter over the top.

Bake for 60–70 minutes. Transfer to a rack to cool.

Chill for 1 hour before serving.

· · ·

If you liked this recipe, you will love these as well.

MINI MILK CHOCOLATE
CHEESECAKES

BLACK FOREST
CHEESECAKE

MARBLED CHEESECAKE

BLACK FOREST CHEESECAKE

1	chocolate crust (see page 342)
7	ounces (200 g) dark chocolate, chopped
2	tablespoons boiling water
1	teaspoon gelatin
1	pound (500 g) cream cheese
1/2	cup (100 g) dark brown sugar
1	(1-pound/500-g) jar morello cherries
2	tablespoons sugar
1	tablespoon cornstarch (cornflour)
	Milk chocolate curls

Prepare the crust following the instructions on page 342.

Melt the chocolate in a double boiler over barely simmering water, or in the microwave. Put the boiling water in a heatproof cup. Sprinkle with the gelatin and stir with a fork until it dissolves.

Beat the cream cheese and brown sugar in a bowl with an electric mixer on medium speed until smooth. Add the chocolate and gelatin mixture, beating until just combined.

Spoon the filling into the crust, smoothing the surface. Chill for 6 hours.

Drain the cherries, reserving the syrup. Combine the sugar and cornstarch in a small saucepan with the reserved syrup. Bring to a boil over medium heat. Remove from the heat, add the cherries, and set aside for 30 minutes to cool.

Serve the cheesecake topped with the cherries and chocolate curls.

Serves: 8–12 Preparation: 20 minutes + 7–8 hours to chill Cooking: 50 minutes Level: 2

DOUBLE CHOCOLATE CHEESECAKE

1	chocolate crust (see page 342)
2/3	cup (150 ml) heavy (double) cream
7	ounces (200 g) dark chocolate
5	ounces (150 g) milk chocolate
14	ounces (400 g) cream cheese
1	pound (500 g) ricotta cheese
1	cup (200 g) sugar
1	teaspoon vanilla extract (essence)
5	large eggs, separated
	Chocolate curls

Prepare the crust following the instructions on page 342. Wrap the outsides of the cooled pan in aluminum foil to make it waterproof.

Heat the cream and both types of chocolate in a double boiler over barely simmering water, stirring until smooth. Set aside to cool a little.

Process the cream cheese, ricotta, sugar, and vanilla in a food processor until smooth. Add the egg yolks one at a time, processing until just combined. Add the chocolate mixture and process until just combined.

Beat the egg whites in a bowl with an electric mixer on medium speed until stiff peaks form. Fold into the chocolate mixture. Pour over the chilled crust and smooth the top.

Place in a roasting pan and pour in enough boiling water to come halfway up the sides of the springform pan. Bake for 1 1/2 hours, until set but still slightly wobbly in the center. Let cool for 1 hour. Chill in the refrigerator overnight. Garnish with chocolate curls. Slice and serve.

Serves: 8–12 Preparation: 30 minutes + 13 hours to cool & chill Cooking: 1 1/2 hours Level: 2

The flavors in this sensational cheesecake are inspired by the famous Black Forest Cake, from southern Germany.

This cheesecake has a lovely, deep chocolate flavor. Serve with tiny cups or glasses of espresso coffee.

Serves: 10-12
Preparation: 40 minutes
    + 13 hours to cool
    & chill
Cooking: 60-70 minutes
Level: 2

· · · · ·

Choose bright and colorful flowers that will contrast with the colors of the cheesecake. Be sure to choose flowers that are non-toxic and have not been sprayed with chemicals.

WHITE LADYFINGER CHEESECAKE
with edible flowers

Crust

2   cups (250 g) ladyfingers (sponge fingers), finely crushed
1/3 cup (90 g) unsalted butter, melted
1   tablespoon unsweetened cocoa powder

Filling

12   ounces (350 g) white chocolate, coarsely chopped
1/2 cup (120 ml) heavy (double) cream
1 1/2 pounds (750 g) cream cheese, softened
3   tablespoons vanilla sugar
4   large eggs
1   tablespoon cornstarch (cornflour)
1   teaspoon almond extract (essence)

Topping

1   cup (250 ml) crème fraîche
2   tablespoons superfine (caster) sugar
1   teaspoon vanilla bean paste or vanilla extract (essence)
    White chocolate curls or flakes for decoration
    Edible flowers, to decorate

Crust: Grease the bottom and sides of a 9-inch (23-cm) springform pan. Preheat the oven to 350°F (180°C/gas 4).

Mix the ladyfinger crumbs with the butter and cocoa in a bowl until well combined. Press firmly into the bottom and up the sides of the prepared pan. Bake for 5 minutes, then set aside to cool. Reduce the oven temperature to 300°F (150°C/gas 2).

Filling: Melt the chocolate and cream in a double boiler over low heat, stirring until smooth. Set aside to cool a little.

Beat the cream cheese and vanilla sugar in a large bowl with an electric mixer on medium speed until smooth. Add the eggs one at a time, beating until just combined after each addition. Mix in the cornstarch. With the mixer on low speed, beat in the chocolate mixture and almond extract. Pour the filling into the crust, leveling the top.

Bake for 45–55 minutes, until the edges are firm but the center is still wobbly. If the top begins to brown, reduce the oven temperature a little. Place on a wire rack.

Increase the oven temperature to 375°F (190°C/gas 5).

Topping: Whisk the crème fraîche, sugar, and vanilla in a bowl, then spoon over the cheesecake. Tilt the pan to distribute evenly. Return to the oven and bake for 10 minutes.

Turn off the oven and leave the cheesecake inside with the door ajar for 1 hour. Refrigerate overnight. Decorate with chocolate curls and flowers. Let sit at room temperature for 15 minutes. Slice and serve.

· · ·

If you liked this recipe, you will love these as well.

242 WHITE CHOCOLATE & RASPBERRY TIRAMISÙ

251 WHITE CHOCOLATE TRIFLE

278 WHITE CHOCOLATE CHEESECAKE WITH RASPBERRY COULIS

Serves: 8

Preparation: 30 minutes
+ 13 hours to cool
& chill

Cooking: 40 minutes

Level: 2

MARBLED CHEESECAKE

Crust

2   cups (250 g) graham cracker or digestive biscuit crumbs

1/2   cup (120 g) unsalted butter, melted

1   tablespoon unsweetened cocoa powder + extra, to dust

Filling

3 1/2   ounces (100 g) dark chocolate, chopped

3/4   cup (180 ml) sour cream or crème fraîche

1   pound (500 g) cream cheese, softened

1   teaspoon vanilla extract (essence)

1   cup (200 g) superfine (caster) sugar

2   tablespoons all-purpose (plain) flour

1   tablespoon finely grated unwaxed orange or lemon zest

3   large eggs

Crust: Grease a 9-inch (23-cm) springform cake pan. Preheat the oven to 350°F (180°C/gas 4).

Mix the cookie crumbs, butter, and cocoa in a bowl with a fork until moist crumbs form. Press firmly into the base and up the sides of the prepared pan. Chill in the refrigerator while you prepare the filling.

Filling: Heat the chocolate and half the sour cream in a double boiler over barely simmering water, stirring until smooth. Set aside to cool.

Beat the cream cheese, vanilla, sugar, and remaining sour cream in a bowl with an electric mixer on medium speed until smooth. Beat in the flour and orange or lemon zest, followed by the eggs. Pour two-thirds of the cream cheese mixture into the chilled crust.

Beat the melted chocolate mixture into the remaining cream cheese mixture until smooth. Spoon the chocolate filling over the vanilla filling.

Bake for 40 minutes, until the center is just firm.

Let cool to room temperature, then chill overnight. Dust with cocoa, slice, and serve.

. . .

If you liked this recipe, you will love these as well.

MILK CHOCOLATE
CHEESECAKE

WHITE CHOCOLATE
CHEESECAKE WITH
RASPBERRY COULIS

BLACK FOREST
CHEESECAKE

candy

Here you will find 18 exquisite recipes
for fudge, chocolate, truffles, and candy.
Try the Chocolate-dipped strawberries
as a healthy snack, or the Truffle
temptation as a sinful dessert.

Makes: 30 pieces
Preparation: 15 minutes
    + 1 hour to set
Cooking: 5 minutes
Level: 1

. . . . .
These strawberries make a healthy and refreshing dessert or snack during the hot summer months.

CHOCOLATE-DIPPED STRAWBERRIES

4   ounces (120 g) dark chocolate, chopped

4   ounces (120 g) white chocolate, chopped

30   large ripe strawberries, stalks on

Line a large baking sheet with parchment paper.

Melt each type of chocolate separately in a double boiler over barely simmering water, or in the microwave. Remove from the heat.

Dip fifteen of the strawberries into the dark chocolate by holding the stalks and lowering the fruit carefully into the chocolate. Turn the fruit in the chocolate, making sure that the chocolate adheres in a smooth layer about two-thirds of the way up the sides of the fruit. Set aside on the prepared baking sheet. Dip again, for an extra thick coating.

Place on the prepared baking sheet and let set at cool room temperature, at least 1 hour.

Repeat with the white chocolate and remaining strawberries.

. . .

If you liked this recipe, you will love these as well.

CHOCOLATE STRAW-
BERRY CUPCAKES

WHITE CHOCOLATE
CUPCAKES WITH
STRAWBERRIES

CHOCOLATE TARTLETS
WITH RASPBERRIES

CHOCOLATE, ORANGE & NUT CANDY

1	unwaxed navel orange
8	ounces (250 g) dark chocolate, chopped
3/4	cup (100 g) hazelnuts, skins removed, coarsely chopped
1/8	teaspoon coarse sea salt

Line a small baking sheet with aluminum foil or parchment paper and place in the refrigerator.

Remove the zest (orange part only) from the orange using a vegetable peeler. Cut the peel into very thin strips about 1 inch (2.5 cm) long using a sharp knife.

Melt the chocolate in a double boiler over barely simmering water, or in the microwave.

Stir in half the orange zest and hazelnuts and immediately pour onto prepared baking sheet. Spread with a rubber spatula into an 8 x 10-inch (20 x 25-cm) rectangle. Sprinkle with the remaining zest, nuts, and salt.

Chill until firm, about 30 minutes. Break into pieces and serve.

Makes: 15–20 pieces Preparation: 15 minutes + 30 minutes to set Cooking: 5 minutes Level: 1

FRUIT & NUT CHOCOLATE CANDY

1/3	cup (40 g) unsalted, shelled pistachios, halved
1/3	cup (60 g) golden raisins (sultanas)
1/3	cup (60 g) slivered almonds
2	tablespoons chopped candied (glacé) orange peel
5	ounces (150 g) milk or dark chocolate, coarsely chopped

Mix the pistachios, golden raisins, almonds, and candied orange peel in a bowl. Set aside.

Melt the chocolate in a double boiler over barely simmering water, or in the microwave. Stir until melted and smooth.

Lay a sheet of parchment paper on a large baking sheet and use a teaspoon to spread 1-inch (2.5-cm) circles of chocolate on the paper.

Quickly decorate the chocolate circles with a mixture of the dried fruit and nuts, then let cool and set, at least 1 hour.

Makes: 16–20 pieces Preparation: 15 minutes + 1 hour to set Cooking: 5 minutes Level: 1

You could also use milk
or white chocolate to
make these chocolate
candies.

Serve these little treats
after dinner with strong
espresso coffee or a
sweet liqueur.

Makes: 16–20 pieces
Preparation: 30 minutes
  + 2 hours to set
Cooking: 15–20 minutes
Level: 1

. . . . .

This is a classic peppermint fudge. If you don't like peppermint with chocolate, replace the peppermint extract with almond extract.

CHOCOLATE PEPPERMINT FUDGE

$^1/_2$ cup (120 g) salted butter, chopped

2 tablespoons glucose syrup

1 (14-ounce/400-g) can sweetened condensed milk

$1^1/_3$ cups (270 g) firmly packed dark brown sugar

7 ounces (200 g) dark chocolate, finely chopped

1 teaspoon peppermint extract (essence)

Grease a 10-inch (25-cm) square cake pan. Line the base and sides with parchment paper, leaving a 1-inch (2.5-cm) overhang on two sides.

Combine the butter, glucose syrup, condensed milk, and brown sugar in a medium saucepan over medium heat. Cook and stir until the sugar is dissolved and the mixture is smooth, 3–5 minutes.

Bring to a rolling boil and continue cooking, without stirring, until the mixture reaches 238°F (118°C) on a candy thermometer, or the soft-ball stage. At this temperature, if you drop a spoonful of the mixture into ice water, it will make a limp, sticky ball that flattens when you remove from the water. Wash down the sides of the pan with a pastry brush dipped in water to stop sugar crystals from forming.

Remove from the heat and quickly stir in the dark chocolate and peppermint until melted and well combined.

Spread the mixture in the prepared pan. Chill until set, at least 2 hours. Cut into squares, and serve.

. . .

If you liked this recipe, you will love these as well.

CHOCOLATE MINT HEARTS

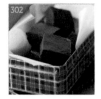

IRISH CREAM FUDGE

CHOCOLATE FUDGE

Makes: 15–20 pieces
Preparation: 20 minutes
    + 45 minutes to set
Cooking: 5 minutes
Level: 2

. . . . .

These mint-flavored hearts are perfect for Valentine's Day of 14 February. Prepare them a day ahead and store in an airtight container in the refrigerator.

CHOCOLATE MINT HEARTS

14   ounces (400 g) dark chocolate, chopped

2½   cups (375 g) confectioners' (icing) sugar

1   tablespoon vegetable oil

1   tablespoons milk, as required

½   teaspoon peppermint extract (essence)

Grease a deep 8-inch (20-cm) square cake pan. Line the base and sides with parchment paper, leaving a 2-inch (5-cm) overhang on all sides.

Place half the chocolate in a microwave-safe bowl. Microwave on high for 1–2 minutes, until smooth, stirring with a metal spoon every 30 seconds. Pour the chocolate over the base of the prepared pan. Chill for 15 minutes, until set.

Sift the confectioners' sugar into a heatproof bowl. Stir in the oil and milk to form a thick paste. Microwave on high for 2–3 minutes, until smooth, stirring every 30 seconds. Stir in the peppermint extract. Set aside for 2 minutes to cool slightly. If the mixture is too thick, stir in an extra tablespoon of milk.

Pour the peppermint mixture over the chocolate in the pan, spreading evenly. Chill for 15 minutes, until just set.

Place the remaining chocolate in a microwave-safe bowl. Microwave on high for 1–2 minutes, until smooth, stirring with a metal spoon every 30 seconds. Pour the chocolate over the peppermint layer. Chill for at least 15 minutes, until just set.

Lift the chocolate from the pan and use a small heart-shaped cookie cutter to cut out the hearts. Roll the scraps into balls.

Chill until ready to serve.

. . .

If you liked this recipe, you will love these as well.

CHOCOLATE PEPPERMINT FUDGE

CHOCOLATE FUDGE

CHOCOLATE PECAN FUDGE

Makes: 35–40 pieces

Preparation: 30 minutes
    + 14–15 hours to chill
    & set

Cooking: 5 minutes

Level: 2

· · · · ·

You could experiment with different coatings, rolling the truffles in finely chopped almonds or finely grated chocolate, or serving in petit-four cases.

TRUFFLE TEMPTATION

Truffles

7	ounces (200 g) bittersweet chocolate (70 % cocoa solids), broken into pieces
3¹/₂	ounces (100 g) dark orange chocolate (55–70 % cocoa solids), broken into pieces
¹/₂	cup (120 ml) heavy (double) cream
1	vanilla pod, split
²/₃	cup (150 g) unsalted butter, softened
2	tablespoons Grand Marnier, rum, or kirsch (optional)
	Unsweetened cocoa powder, to dust hands

To Coat

3¹/₂	ounces (100 g) white chocolate, chopped
3¹/₂	ounces (100 g) bittersweet chocolate, chopped
4	tablespoons finely chopped pistachios

Truffles: Melt both chocolates in a double boiler over barely simmering water, or in the microwave.

Heat the cream with the vanilla pod in a small saucepan, and boil gently for 2 minutes. Leave to cool. Remove the vanilla pod and mix the cooled cream with the melted chocolate, beating until completely combined.

Beat the butter in a large mixing bowl with an electric mixer at high speed for 2–3 minutes, until very creamy and light. Beat the chocolate and cream mixture into the butter, a large spoonful at a time. Whisk in the Grand Marnier. Continue beating until smooth and glossy. Leave to set at room temperature for 50–60 minutes. Do not chill in the refrigerator, as the truffle mixture will be too firm to roll.

Place a large baking sheet with parchment paper. Dust your hands with cocoa, take a teaspoon of the mixture, and roll it into a marble-sized ball. Repeat with the remaining mixture. Place on the baking sheet and chill in the refrigerator until set, about 2 hours.

To Coat: Melt the chocolates in separate double boilers over barely simmering water, or in separate bowls in the microwave. Remove from the heat and stir until smooth.

Spear a truffle with a toothpick and dip into the chocolate. Place on clean parchment paper, spacing well apart. Slip the truffles off the toothpicks with a second toothpick. Repeat until all the truffles are coated with chocolate.

Put the pistachios in a shallow bowl. Roll some of the dark truffles in the bowl. Place on a plate, keep in a cool place for 30 minutes, and then chill overnight.

CHOCOLATE ORANGE TRUFFLES

12	ounces (350 g) dark chocolate, coarsely chopped
1/2	cup (120 ml) heavy (double) cream
2	tablespoons orange liqueur
1/2	cup (75 g) Dutch-process cocoa, sifted, to dust

Put the chocolate in a heatproof bowl.

Heat the cream in a small, heavy-based saucepan and bring almost to a boil. Pour over the chocolate. Let stand for 5 minutes, then stir until smooth. Stir in the liqueur.

Let cool to room temperature, then chill until the mixture is firm, at least 4 hours, or overnight.

Scoop up a teaspoon of chilled chocolate, and quickly roll into a ball. Continue until the mixture is used up. Roll each truffle in cocoa to coat. Chill until firm.

Makes: 20–25 truffles Preparation: 20 minutes + 4-12 hours to chill Cooking: 5 minutes Level: 1

COCONUT TRUFFLES

8	ounces (250 g) dark chocolate, coarsely chopped
1	cup (250 ml) heavy (double) cream
1 1/3	cups (200 g) unsweetened shredded (desiccated) coconut

Put the chocolate in a heatproof bowl.

Heat the cream in a small, heavy-based saucepan and bring almost to a boil. Pour over the chocolate. Let stand for 5 minutes, then stir until smooth.

Let cool to room temperature, then chill until the mixture is firm, at least 4 hours, or overnight.

Scoop out teaspoons of the mixture and roll into balls with your hands.

Put the coconut on a plate and roll the truffles in it until evenly coated. Cover and keep in the refrigerator until ready to serve.

Makes: 20–25 truffles Preparation: 20 minutes + 4-12 hours to set Cooking: 5 minutes Level: 1

If serving these truffles to children, you may prefer to replace the orange liqueur with orange flower water.

These truffles make a wonderful treat for coconut lovers.

Makes: 16–20 pieces

Preparation: 10 minutes
    + 5 hours to cool
    & chill

Cooking: 20 minutes

Level: 1

IRISH CREAM FUDGE

1   (14-ounce/400-g)
     can sweetened
     condensed milk

1/3 cup (90 g) salted
     butter, cubed

1¼   cups (250 g) firmly
     packed brown sugar

2   tablespoons glucose
     syrup

5   ounces (150 g) dark
     chocolate, finely
     chopped

1/4 cup (60 ml) Baileys
     Irish Cream liqueur

Lightly grease an 8-inch (20-cm) square cake pan with melted butter.

Combine the condensed milk, butter, brown sugar, and glucose syrup in a medium, heavy-based saucepan. Stir over medium-low heat for 3–4 minutes, until the sugar dissolves.

Bring to a rolling boil and continue cooking, without stirring, until the mixture reaches 238°F (118°C) on a candy thermometer, or the soft-ball stage. At this temperature, if you drop a spoonful of the mixture into ice water, it will make a limp, sticky ball that flattens when you remove from the water. Wash down the sides of the pan with a pastry brush dipped in water to stop sugar crystals from forming.

Remove from the heat. Add the chocolate and liqueur, and stir until the chocolate melts and the mixture is smooth.

Pour into the prepared pan, smoothing the surface. Set aside for 1 hour to cool.

Cover with plastic wrap (cling film) and chill in the refrigerator for at least 4 hours. Use a sharp knife to cut the fudge into 16–20 equal pieces.

. . .

*If you liked this recipe,
you will love these as well.*

CHOCOLATE
PEPPERMINT FUDGE

CHOCOLATE PECAN
FUDGE

WHITE CHOCOLATE
WALNUT FUDGE

Makes: 16–20 pieces

Preparation: 30 minutes
    + 3 hours to cool
    & set

Cooking: 15–20 minutes

Level: 1

CHOCOLATE FUDGE

3	cups (600 g) sugar
2	tablespoons unsweetened cocoa powder
1/4	teaspoon salt
3	tablespoons light corn (golden) syrup
1	cup (250 ml) milk
4	ounces (120 g) dark chocolate, finely chopped
1/3	cup (90 g) unsalted butter, cut into small pieces
2	teaspoons vanilla extract (essence)

Butter an 8-inch (20-cm) square baking pan. Line with parchment paper. Butter a large, shallow, stainless-steel bowl.

Combine the sugar, cocoa, and salt in a large, heavy-based saucepan. Place over medium-low heat, and add corn syrup and milk, stirring until smooth. Add the chocolate. Cook, stirring constantly, until the chocolate is melted and the sugar is dissolved.

Bring to a rolling boil and continue cooking, without stirring, until the mixture reaches 238°F (118°C) on a candy thermometer, or the soft-ball stage. At this temperature, if you drop a spoonful of the mixture into ice water, it will make a limp, sticky ball that flattens when you remove from the water. Wash down the sides of the pan with a pastry brush dipped in water to stop sugar crystals from forming.

Pour into the prepared bowl and dot with the butter. Let cool almost to room temperature without stirring, about 1 hour. Add the vanilla.

Transfer to the bowl of an electric mixer. Using the paddle attachment, beat on low speed until the butter and vanilla are well incorporated. Increase the speed to medium, and beat until the fudge keeps its shape when dropped from a spoon and the sheen is gone.

Transfer to the prepared baking pan, spreading evenly. Before the fudge sets completely, score with a knife into 1-inch (2.5-cm) squares. Let stand until completely cool, at least 2 hours.

. . .

If you liked this recipe, you will love these as well.

IRISH CREAM FUDGE

WHITE CHOCOLATE WALNUT FUDGE

WALNUT FUDGE SQUARES

Makes: 30–32 pieces
Preparation: 30 minutes
    + 4–12 hours to chill
    & set
Cooking: 15–20 minutes
Level: 1

. . . . .

You can easily convert this fudge to a walnut, almond, or macadamia flavor by simply replacing the pecans with the same quantity of any of these nuts.

CHOCOLATE PECAN FUDGE

4	cups (800 g) sugar
1/2	cup (75 g) Dutch-process cocoa powder
1 1/2	cups (375 ml) heavy (double) cream
1/2	cup (120 g) unsalted butter
3	tablespoons light corn (golden) syrup
2	teaspoons vanilla extract (essence)
1 1/2	cups (200 g) chopped pecans + extra, to decorate

Mix the sugar and cocoa in a medium, heavy-based saucepan. Add the cream, butter, and corn syrup and simmer over medium-high heat, stirring, until bubbling around the edges, about 5 minutes.

Bring to a rolling boil and continue cooking, without stirring, until the mixture reaches 238°F (118°C) on a candy thermometer, or the soft-ball stage. At this temperature, if you drop a spoonful of the mixture into ice water, it will make a limp, sticky ball that flattens when you remove from the water. Wash down the sides of pan with a pastry brush dipped in water to stop sugar crystals from forming.

Remove the pan from the heat. Let the fudge rest in the pan, without stirring, until almost at room temperature.

Line a large baking sheet with parchment paper.

Add the vanilla and stir the fudge until you see a sudden change in its appearance, from glossy to matte. Sprinkle with the chopped pecans and stir well to combine.

Spread the fudge on the prepared baking sheet. Cover with another sheet of parchment paper. Let stand at room temperature until set, at least 4 hours, or overnight.

Cut into squares and press a pecan half into each one before serving.

. . .

If you liked this recipe, you will love these as well.

TRUFFLE TEMPTATION

WHITE CHOCOLATE
WALNUT FUDGE

WALNUT FUDGE
SQUARES

Makes: 30 pieces

Preparation: 30 minutes
+ 12 hours to
macerate & 12 hours
to set

Cooking: 5 minutes

Level: 2

These chocolate cherry delights look so pretty served in tiny petit-four cases.

CHOCOLATE CHERRY DELIGHTS

30 candied (glacé) cherries

5   tablespoons cherry brandy

8   ounces (250 g) dark chocolate

Macerate the cherries in the brandy in a small bowl overnight. Drain the cherries, discarding the brandy.

Melt the chocolate in a double boiler over barely simmering water, or in the microwave.

Spoon or pipe the chocolate into tiny foil or paper petit-four or mini muffin cases, filling each one almost to the top. Place a cherry in each case.

Let set, about 12 hours. Arrange in a serving dish, and serve.

. . .

If you liked this recipe, you will love these as well.

CHOCOLATE ORANGE TRUFFLES

CHOCOLATE EASTER EGGS WITH SPRINKLES

CHOCOLATE POPCORN

Makes: about 30 pieces
Preparation: 30 minutes
    + 3–4 hours to cool
    & chill
Cooking: 15–20 minutes
Level: 1

WHITE CHOCOLATE WALNUT FUDGE

1   cup (250 g) salted
     butter
1¹/₂ cups (375 ml) milk
2¹/₂ cups (500 g) sugar
4   ounces (120 g) white
     chocolate, finely
     chopped
1   cup (120 g) walnuts,
     chopped
1   teaspoon vanilla
     extract (essence)

Oil an 8 x 10-inch (20 x 25-cm) baking pan. Place the butter, milk, and sugar in a saucepan over medium heat. Stir until the sugar is dissolved.

Bring to a rolling boil and continue cooking, without stirring, until the mixture reaches 238°F (118°C) on a candy thermometer, or the soft-ball stage. At this temperature, if you drop a spoonful of the mixture into ice water, it will make a limp, sticky ball that flattens when you remove from the water. Wash down the sides of the pan with a pastry brush dipped in water to stop sugar crystals from forming.

Remove from the heat and beat until the fudge starts to thicken, about 5 minutes. Add the chocolate and stir until it has melted. Stir in the walnuts and vanilla extract.

Pour the mixture into the prepared pan. Let cool to room temperature, about 1 hour. Chill in the refrigerator until set, 2–3 hours.

Cut into squares and serve.

. . .

If you liked this recipe, you will love these as well.

TRUFFLE TEMPTATION

CHOCOLATE PECAN
TOFFEE

CHOCOLATE EASTER
EGGS WITH SPRINKLES

WALNUT FUDGE SQUARES

3/4 cup (180 ml) sweetened condensed milk
12 ounces (350 g) dark chocolate, coarsely grated
2 tablespoons unsalted butter, softened
28 walnut halves

Butter a shallow 7 x 11-inch (18 x 28-cm) baking pan with butter.

Warm the condensed milk in a heavy-based saucepan over low heat for 2–3 minutes, stirring constantly. Add the chocolate and butter, and continue stirring until the chocolate has melted and the mixture is smooth.

Remove the saucepan from the heat and pour into the prepared pan. Leave to cool, and when the fudge is firm enough, cut into squares and decorate each one with a walnut half.

When completely cool and set, about 4 hours, remove from the pan, and serve.

Makes: about 28 pieces Preparation: 10 minutes + 4 hours to set Cooking: 10 minutes Level: 1

CHOCOLATE PECAN TOFFEE

1 1/2 cups (200 g) broken pecans
1 cup (250 g) unsalted butter
1/2 cup (100 g) sugar
2 cups (400 g) firmly packed light brown sugar
1/2 teaspoon salt
2 cups (350 g) dark chocolate chips

Preheat the oven to 350°F (180°C/gas 4). Line a 10 x 15-inch (25 x 38-cm) baking pan with aluminum foil. Butter the foil. Spread the pecans evenly over the foil.

Place the butter, both types of sugar, and the salt in a heavy-based saucepan over medium heat. Bring to a rolling boil, stirring constantly.

Spoon the sugar mixture over the pecans to coat. Bake for 10 minutes, until bubbly all over the surface. Immediately sprinkle with the chocolate chips.

Let cool in the pan for 10 minutes, then score the top with a knife into 1-inch (2.5-cm) squares. Let cool completely, at least 1 hour.

Peel off the foil, break the toffee into pieces along the scorelines, and serve.

Makes: about 36 pieces Preparation: 15 minutes + 1 hour to cool Cooking: 15–20 minutes Level: 1

If liked, you could coarsely chop an extra ½ cup (60 g) of walnuts and stir them into the fudge mixture.

This delicious chocolate-coated toffee makes a perfect pick-me-up with a cup of espresso coffee.

Makes: about 20 eggs
Preparation: 30 minutes
    + 2–3 hours to chill
Cooking: 5 minutes
Level: 2

CHOCOLATE EASTER EGGS
with sprinkles

1½ pounds (750 g) dark chocolate, chopped

¾ cup (180 ml) heavy (double) cream

¼ cup (60 g) salted butter

2 cups colored sprinkles to finish

Heat 1¼ pounds (600 g) of the chocolate with the cream and butter in a double boiler over barely simmering water. Stir occasionally until the mixture is smooth and shiny.

Pour the mixture into a shallow container and cover with plastic wrap (cling film). Chill in the refrigerator until cold and firm, 1–2 hours.

Using your hands, roll teaspoons of the chocolate mixture into balls, placing them on a platter ready for finishing. Chill in the refrigerator for 1 hour.

Melt the remaining chocolate in a double boiler over barely simmering water, or in the microwave. Put the sprinkles in a bowl.

Spear each egg with a toothpick and dip it in the chocolate and then immediately roll it in the sprinkles. Repeat with all the eggs. Make sure they are all thoroughly coated in the sprinkles.

Arrange on a serving platter, and serve.

. . .

If you liked this recipe, you will love these as well.

CHOCOLATE CHERRY DELIGHTS

CHOCOLATE PECAN TOFFEE

CHOCOLATE HOKEY POKEY

CHOCOLATE HOKEY POKEY

5 tablespoons (60 g) sugar

2 tablespoons corn (golden) syrup

1 teaspoon baking soda (bicarbonate of soda)

8 ounces (250 g) bittersweet or dark chocolate

Butter a 9-inch (23-cm) square baking pan.

Combine the sugar and corn syrup in a medium, heavy-based saucepan over low heat. Stirring constantly, bring to a gentle boil. Simmer for 4 minutes, stirring often.

Remove from the heat and stir in the baking soda. The mixture will bubble up, quickly doubling or tripling in volume. Working rapidly, pour into the prepared pan. Let cool to room temperature.

Melt the chocolate in a double boiler over barely simmering water. Let cool for 5 minutes. Remove the toffee from the pan and break or cut into bite-size pieces. Using tongs, dip the pieces into the chocolate, swirling to coat well. Place on a baking sheet.

Let set for at least 30 minutes before serving.

Makes: 20–30 pieces Preparation: 20 minutes + 30 minutes to set Cooking: 5 minutes Level: 1

CHOCOLATE POPCORN

1 tablespoon sunflower oil

4 tablespoons (75 g) unpopped popcorn

14 ounces (400 g) dark chocolate

2 ounces (60 g) white chocolate

Line a large baking sheet with parchment paper.

Heat the oil in a large heavy-based saucepan over medium heat.

When hot, add the popcorn, cover quickly with the lid, and cook until all the corn has popped, shaking the pan lightly during cooking for even popping.

Melt both chocolates separately in double boilers over barely simmering water. Pour the popped corn into the dark chocolate and stir until well coated. Spread out on the prepared baking sheet and drizzle with the white chocolate. Leave to set, about 1 hour.

Makes: 40–50 pieces Preparation: 20 minutes Cooking: 15 minutes Level: 1

Hokey pokey is also known as honeycomb toffee in many parts of the world. Light and chewy, this chocolate-covered version tastes just like a homemade Crunchie bar.

Chocolate-coated popcorn makes a great snack for watching movies at home. You could also coat the popcorn in milk chocolate, if preferred.

index